T0332684

Big Data
A Tutorial-Based Approach

Big Data
A Tutorial-Based Approach

Nasir Raheem

CRC Press
Taylor & Francis Group
Boca Raton London New York

CRC Press is an imprint of the
Taylor & Francis Group, an **informa** business

CRC Press
Taylor & Francis Group
6000 Broken Sound Parkway NW, Suite 300
Boca Raton, FL 33487-2742

© 2019 by Taylor & Francis Group, LLC
CRC Press is an imprint of Taylor & Francis Group, an Informa business

No claim to original U.S. Government works

ISBN-13: 978-0-367-18345-5 (hbk)

Library of Congress Cataloging-in-Publication Data

Names: Raheem, Nasir, author.
Title: Big data : a tutorial-based approach / Nasir Raheem.
Description: First edition. | Boca Raton, FL : Taylor & Francis
Group, [2019] | Includes bibliographical references and index.
Identifiers: LCCN 2018060975| ISBN 9780367183455 (hardback :
acid-free paper) | ISBN 9780429060939 (ebook)
Subjects: LCSH: Big data--Programmed instruction.
Classification: LCC QA76.9.B45 R34 2019 | DDC 005.7--dc23
LC record available at https://lccn.loc.gov/2018060975

**Visit the Taylor & Francis Web site at
http://www.taylorandfrancis.com**

**and the CRC Press Web site at
http://www.crcpress.com**

*Dedicated to my wife, Saba, for
her support and endurance.*

Contents

List of Tutorials

List of Figures/ Illustrations

Foreword

It is a pleasure for me to present my introductory remarks. After reviewing the book, I felt this book will impact the reader in several ways:

1. A well thought-out guide comprising tutorials and graphic illustrations that builds an integrated approach which clearly answers the "What" and the "How" and the "Why" of "Big Data."

2. It takes the readers on an inquisitive journey through the information wonderland of Data Lakes and provides the tools and techniques to bring about the marriage of structured and un-structured data.

3. It is a must-read primer that keeps its eyes always set on the end goal of extracting useful business insight from "Big Data" by fully exploiting the potential of Hadoop Distributed File System Infrastructure, MapReduce processing, and Agile Data Analytics to implement proper Data Migration, Data Ingestion, Data Management, Data Analytics, Data Visualization, and Data Virtualization processes.

4. Last, but not the least, this book finally tests the readers on their understanding of "Big Data" in the form of a QUIZ.

Sohail Subhani
MIS Professor
College of Business
Winona State University

Preface

I was inspired to write a book on Big Data after the publication of my online course by Harvard University Innovation Lab platform, experfy.com. This course is hosted at: https://www.experfy.com/training/courses/march-towards-big-data-big-data-implementation-migration-ingestion-management-visualization.

Essentially, this kindled a long-time desire to write a book that will serve as a guide and answer the key questions, "What," "How," and "Why" of "Big Data." I envisioned this book to comprise tutorials that will help navigate through the information wonderland and lead to the end goal of extracting useful business insight from "Big Data."

In addition to my experience in business intelligence, data architecture, and IT infrastructure, I had to draw upon technical white papers, innumerable blogs, and operating manuals to share the state-of-the-art tutorials with my readers. These tutorials relate to data migration, data ingestion, data management, data visualization, and data virtualization processes.

Gartner, IBM, Accenture, and many others have asserted that 80% or more of the world's information is un-structured – and inherently hard to analyze. What does that mean? And what is required to extract insight from un-structured data?

First, we need to understand un-structured data. It is infinitely variable in quality and format, because it is produced by humans who can be unpredictable and ill-informed, but always unique in their own way, that is, not standard in any way. Recent advances in natural language processing provide the notion that un-structured content can be included in modern day data analytics. There is a realm of R programming that can be used for this purpose.

Natural language processing, as in R programming, results in text analytics as a way to gain business value from un-structured data. Data visualization and data virtualization tools provide the process of analyzing un-structured text stored in Big Data repositories, extracting relevant information, and transforming it into structured digital information that can then be leveraged in various ways. The analysis and extraction processes take advantage of techniques that originated in computational linguistics, statistics, and other computer science disciplines such as business intelligence and artificial intelligence.

To get the most business value from our real-time analysis of un-structured data, we need to understand the data in context with our historical data on customers, products, transactions, and operations. This real-time analysis has supported the emergence of Fast, Wide, and Deep (3-D) dashboards that provide insight into "data we don't know that we need to know." In other words, we will need to integrate text analytics of the un-structured data in real time with traditional operational data.

Now, why is this important? It is because serious growth and value companies are committed to data. The exponential growth of Big Data has posed major challenges in data management, data governance, and data analytics. Good data management, data governance, and data analytics are pivotal for business growth.

It is of paramount importance, therefore, to slice and dice Big Data that addresses data management, data governance, and issues of data analytics. To support high-quality business decision making, it is important to fully capture the potential of Big Data. This is done by focusing on "Big Data Use Case" that puts to use the latest technology which utilizes Distributed Storage, Efficient, and Fault-Tolerant Parallel Processing.

The end goal of extracting useful business insight from Big Data is achievable by fully harnessing the potential of Hadoop

Distributed File System Infrastructure, MapReduce Processing, and Agile Text Analytics. The Tools and Techniques of Hadoop Eco system serve as effective mechanisms to implement proper Data Migration, Data Ingestion, Data Management, Data Analytics, Data Visualization, and Data Virtualization processes and procedures.

In this book, I have tried my best to live up to the high standards of effectively slicing and dicing Big Data. It is in your hands now and you are the best judge.

Acknowledgements

I would like to thank my publisher, Taylor & Francis, for their careful and thorough review of the manuscript, and my daughter, Nor Raheem, a Graphics Design and Media Arts & Animation professional for her effort in transforming Internet figures into higher-resolution and more artistic illustrations.

I am also grateful to the following persons/group for providing the source of information that was much needed in the development of this book:

1. Philip Russom for his research paper on "Business Value of Big Data."

2. H. Kagermann, W. Wahister and J. Helbig for their research on Digital Transformation of the Production Model.

3. Daniel G. Murray for his research on Visual Analysis in the Tableau toolset.

4. Kelly Black for the tutorial on R programming language.

5. Gartner Group for their insightful white papers.

6. TIBCO for its research on fast, wide and deep dashboards.

7. Andrew O'Connell and Walter Frick for their research on the topic, "From Data to Action."

8. David Stodder for explaining key features of Data Virtualization.

I am also thankful to the big Information Technology firms such as Cloudera, Informatica, Tableau, and Denodo for their online training material and tutorials related to Installation, Configuration, Upgrade, and Testing.

Author

Nasir Raheem performed his graduate work in Management Science and Engineering at Stanford University, California. He's an Oracle Certified Professional (DBA Track), Certified Project Management Professional, Certified Scrum Master, and a Certified Big Data Analyst. He's an experienced manager and architect of IT projects related to multi-billion dollar corporate mergers and divestiture, application migration, server upgrades, database upgrades, data conversion, cloning, and integration of supply chain management, ERP and CRM application modules at Electronic Arts, Wells Fargo Bank, NetApp, Hitachi Global Storage Technologies (now Western Digital), Hewlett Packard, Amazon/Lab126, and Albertsons. In the key role of Data Integrator for multi-billion dollar corporate mergers and divestiture, he has implemented hyperconverged infrastructure from concept to business realization comprising Web Application Servers, Load Balancers, Massive Big Data Databases running on Hadoop clusters, SAN storage, and interconnected commodity servers.

CHAPTER 1

Introduction to Big Data

OVERVIEW

The tidal wave of Big Data is here (see Figure 1.1). We are going to learn how to slice and dice it and start making superior business decisions, learn how to make digital transformation to extract business value out of Big Data, master the journey from structured data processing to natural language processing of un-structured data, and learn how to visualize Big Data in Data Lakes to foster comprehensive business decision making.

RAPID GROWTH OF BIG DATA

Advances in sensor, cloud computing, and machine learning technologies are transforming industry and business models.

The primary drivers of Big Data are:

1. Cloud computing that provides a high level of cybersecurity and data governance;

2. Clustered servers that support distributed processing and thereby provide fault-tolerant and distributed services;

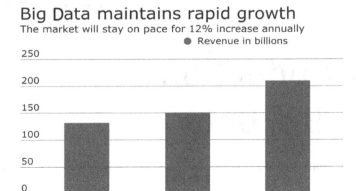

Source: International Data Corp.

FIGURE 1.1 Big Data maintains rapid growth. (From information-management.com.)

3. Internet of Things (IoT) that generates massive amounts of click-stream data that supports machine learning;

4. Clustered servers that utilize hyperconverged architecture which provides high-performance compute, network and storage infrastructure.

The health care industry itself is experiencing high growth, and tops most others in Big Data adoption.

Why Big Data? Big Data plays an important role in the health care industry for the following reasons:

1. They are inundated in large amounts of structured, semi-structured and un-structured data which are analyzed in medical research to provide lifesaving diagnoses and treatment options;

2. They need to provide fast, efficient, and distributed processing;

3. They need to implement strict cybersecurity measures and identity management practices as in cloud computing.

BIG DATA DEFINITION

It is important to understand what Big Data is. Big Data is a term that describes the large volume of data – whether structured (e.g., Relational databases), semi-structured (e.g., Key – value pairs as in Mongo databases), or un-structured (e.g., emails, text files, log files, videos etc.) that inundates a business on a day-to-day basis. But it's not the amount of data that's important; it is what organizations do with that data that matters. Big Data can be analyzed for insights that lead to better decisions and strategic business moves.

In essence, raw Big Data is the sum of structured, semi-structured, and un-structured data. In today's computing world, data is information that has been translated into a form that is efficient for movement or processing. In other words, data is information converted into binary digital form.

Collecting raw Big Data into a Data Lake is one thing, but finding the business value hidden in heaps of structured, semi-structured, and un-structured data is quite another. The challenge is how to extract business value.

We recognize that there is tremendous business value hidden in raw Big Data. However, in order to produce high value information, what is needed is the processing of this raw Big Data which will apply business rules and quality assurance rules to it. It is this valuable information that drives business intelligence, which is so critical for business growth.

Obviously, this large volume of complex data requires a thorough implementation framework.

There are three aspects of Big Data implementation (see Figure 1.2):

1. Tools & Techniques

2. Infrastructure

3. Processing

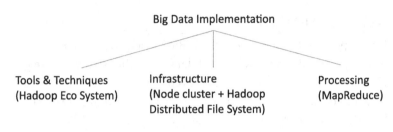

FIGURE 1.2   Big Data implementation.

BIG DATA PROJECTS

Technology and business conditions are ripe for Big Data projects. Technology companies are joining hands to develop powerful solutions! A case in point: Cisco in partnership with NetApp has developed a unified computing, network, and storage infrastructure comprised of Cisco Unified Computing System (UCS) and clustered storage architecture that uses NetApp Fabric Attached Storage (FAS). These systems simplify data management, thereby enabling enterprise customers to reduce costs and complexity, minimize risks, and control change.

The nature of Big Data is data whose scale, diversity, and complexity require new architecture, techniques, and algorithms to manage and extract hidden knowledge from it. The majority of Big Data projects fall into one of two broad categories:

- Storage driven

    - For organizations running corporate internal applications in a private data center that are now faced with large volumes of structured and un-structured data, an in-house Hadoop infrastructure is well suited to what would primarily be data storage driven projects.

- Application driven

    - These primarily use fast and distributed processing as in health care applications. These are those companies that provide promise and potential involved in Big Data analytics where processing speed, such as provided by Agile Data Analytics, is of primary concern. These projects will integrate with cloud providers' security measures – starting by integrating the Big Data platform with the encryption and security practices inherent in the cloud environment. Here, it will be important to offer a centralized control panel to manage data governance. Organizations can take further steps to implement proper Identity Management to minimize access issues.

It is important to use the right tool for the job at hand. Seventy-six percent of organizations actively leverage at least three Big Data open source engines for data preparation, machine learning, and reporting and analysis workloads (e.g., Apache Hadoop/HIVE, Apache Spark, and Presto). Greater productivity and automation is a priority. The statistical data shows that as the size of implementations grow, data-driven companies constantly seek to improve the ratio of users per administrator, thereby reducing the incremental cost of growth and increasing user self-sufficiency.[1]

BUSINESS VALUE OF BIG DATA

We need to understand that earlier systems catered to small to mid-size structured data that lent itself well to business intelligence deliverables such as data mining and ad hoc queries or batch reporting. The new compute, network, and storage capabilities, Mahout tool to facilitate machine learning, and real-time data exploration discovery and predictive analysis have provided deeper insights into business operations data in the form of fast, wide, and deep (3-D) dashboards. Additionally, the new tools and techniques of Hadoop Eco System support optimizations and predictive analysis including complex statistical analysis.

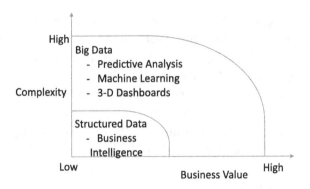

FIGURE 1.3   Business value of Big Data.

Let us look at a pictorial representation (see Figure 1.3) of the business value of Big Data. We observe that Big Data is at the high ends of both business value and complexity.

We will refer to the research paper authored by Philip Russom on "Business Value of Big Data," as this work is of a pioneering nature and we will summarize the findings point-wise. There are nine ways to extract maximum value from Big Data:[2]

- **The primary path to business value is through analytics.** Note that this involves advanced forms of analytics such as those based on data mining, statistical analysis, natural language processing, and extreme SQL. Unlike reporting and OLAP, these enable data exploration and discovery analytics with Big Data. Even so, reporting and OLAP won't go away because they are still valuable elsewhere.

- **Explore Big Data to discover new business opportunities.** After all, many sources of Big Data are new to us, and many represent new channels for interacting with our customers and partners. As with any new source, Big Data merits exploration. Data exploration leads to patterns and new facts our business didn't know, such as new customer base segments, customer behaviors, forms of churn, and root causes for bottom line costs.

- **Start analyzing the Big Data one has already hoarded.** Yes, it's true: many firms have "squirreled away" large datasets because they sensed business value yet didn't know how to get value out of Big Data. Depending on our industry, we probably have large datasets of website logs, which can be "sessionized" and analyzed to understand website visitor behavior. Likewise, quality assurance data from manufacturing leads to more reliable products and better leverage with suppliers, and radio-frequency identification (RFID) data can solve the mysteries of product movement through supply chains.

- **Focus on analyzing the type of Big Data that's valuable to one's industry.** The type and content of Big Data can vary by industry and thus have different value propositions for each industry. This includes call detail records (CDRs) in telecommunications, RFID in retail, manufacturing, and other product-oriented industries, as well as sensor data from robots in manufacturing (especially automotive and consumer electronics).

- **Make a leap of faith into un-structured Big Data.** This information is largely text expressing human language, which is very different from the relational data we work with the most. So, we will need new tools on natural language processing, search, and text analytics. These can provide visibility into text-laden business processes such as the claims process in insurance, medical records in health care, call-center and help-desk applications in any industry, and sentiment analysis in customer-oriented businesses.

- **Expand our existing customer analytics with social media data.** Customers can influence each other by commenting on brands, reviewing products, reacting to marketing campaigns, and revealing shared interests. Social Big Data can come from social media websites as well as from our own channels that enable customers to voice opinions and facts. It's possible to use predictive analytics to discover patterns and anticipate product or service issues. We might likewise measure share of voice, brand reputation, sentiment drivers, and new customer segments.

- **Complete our customer views by integrating Big Data into them.** Big Data (when integrated with older enterprise sources) can broaden 360° views of customers and other business entities (products, suppliers, partners), from hundreds of attributes to thousands. The added granular detail leads to more accurate customer base segmentation, direct marketing, and other customer analytics.

- **Improve older analytic applications by incorporating Big Data.** Big Data can enlarge and broaden data samples for older analytic applications. This is especially the case with analytic technologies that depend on large samples, such as statistics or data mining, when applied to fraud detection, risk management, or actuarial calculations.

- **Accelerate the business into real-time operation by analyzing streaming Big Data which is now made possible by Kafka stream processing.** Applications for real-time monitoring and analysis have been around for many years in businesses that offer an energy utility, communication network, or any grid, service, or facility that demands 24 × 7 operation. More recently, a wider range of organizations are tapping streaming Big Data for applications ranging from surveillance (cybersecurity, situational awareness, fraud detection) to logistics (truck or rail freight, mobile asset management, just-in-time inventory). Big Data analytics is still mostly executed in batch and offline today, but it will move into real time as users and technologies mature.

CHAPTER 2

Big Data Implementation

OVERVIEW

Due to the complexity and volume of Big Data, it is important to take a top-down approach for implementing all of the tools and techniques that comprehensively support the batch processing as well as agile analytics needed to slice and dice Big Data. The top-down approach facilitates building a high-level view of installing the toolset comprised of data ingestion, data management, data storage, data visualization, and data analytics tools.

We need to address the Big Data challenge. This leads us to two school of thoughts.

- The first one is where real-time queries and random access are not required. This approach uses *Data Mining*, which handles time-consuming data processing, mining, and prognosis on large amounts of passive data. It is dependent on Extract/Transform/Load (ETL)/MapReduce batch processing to store data in data marts for further data analysis.

- The second school of thought is that of agile analytics. This depends on *Entity Access,* which performs ad hoc queries on entity data available in Data Lakes for operative decision-making. This requires Big Data solutions that support real-time queries and random access and may use web services like SOAP (Simple Object Access Protocol; it is a messaging protocol used by the web service) or REST (Representational State Transfer; it is a messaging protocol used by the web service which considers unique URL as a representation of an object and does not need to parse the XML configuration file to get the details). This approach bypasses the time-consuming Extract/Transform/Load (ETL) process of staging data in data marts for further data analysis.

HIGH-LEVEL TASKS TO IMPLEMENT INFORMATICA BDM, CLOUDERA HIVE, AND TABLEAU

Install Cloudera Software in Oracle VM Virtual Box (refer to Figure 2.9: Cloudera Software Distribution Bundle).

Set up and configure Informatica BDM with Hadoop.

Create Cloudera HIVE tables and analytics data on Hadoop.

Install Tableau Server; set up and test connection with Hadoop

Implement Informatica Web Intelligence Dashboard in Tableau.

A summary of high-level tasks to set up Informatica BDM, Cloudera HIVE, and Tableau has been presented in the previous text. Essentially, it comprises of 3 layers.

- The visualization and analytics layer – Tableau

  Includes analytic, visualization, and virtualization tools used for statistical analyses, machine learning, predictive analytics, and data exploration. Here, user experience is key. Business users, analysts, and scientists need to be able to quickly and easily query data, test hypotheses, and visualize their findings, preferably in familiar spreadsheet-like interfaces.

- The Big Data management layer – Informatica BDM

  Includes core tools to integrate, govern, and secure Big Data such as pre-built connectors and transformations, data quality, data lineage, and data masking such as Data Vault. Here, the emphasis should be on ensuring data is made fit-for-purpose and protected in an automated, flexible, and scalable way that speeds up the build.

- The data storage layer – Cloudera HIVE

  Includes storage persistence technologies and distributed processing frameworks like Hadoop/MapReduce, Spark, and Cassandra. Here, the emphasis should primarily be on cost reduction and leveraging the linear scalability these technologies enable.

BIG DATA TRIGGERS DIGITAL TRANSFORMATION OF THE PRODUCTION MODEL

To remain competitive under the current conditions of growth in cloud computing, the emergence of clustered servers and Internet of Things (IoT) digital transformation of the industry is in process.

What that means is in addition to the factory of the past, we need to connect the factory to the following new components in the company's production model, also referred to as the solution components of Industry 4.0 (Kagermann et al., 2013).[3]

1. Cloud computing that provides decentralized services as well as a high level of cybersecurity and data governance;

2. Big Data solutions made up of clustered servers that support Hadoop/MapR processing and thereby provide fault-tolerant and distributed services; and

3. IoT as the communication platform that generates massive amounts of click-stream data that supports machine learning (Figure 2.1).

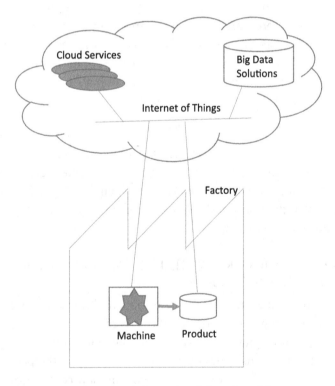

FIGURE 2.1 Convergence of physical and digital worlds.

BIG DATA CHALLENGES AND ASSOCIATED USE CASES

We will cover a wide range of Industry 4.0 data processing requirements. We see four issues requiring high-performance processing
of large data volumes and appropriate Big Data approaches:[4]

1. *Large and continuously growing amount of data*: The
   comprehensive data integration (vertical, horizontal, lifecycle)
   generates Big Data to access and process. The data is comprised
   of active data (e.g., status and description of entities in the
   operative production) and growing passive or past data from
   the lifecycle of entities (e.g., sensor data from machines).

2. *Knowledge processing*: Processing of a large and complex amount
   of past data (e.g., sensor data) for analytics, mining, and
   prognosis to enhance decision making and for optimization.

3. *Random access on data*: Individual situations and events in
   production are triggered to build ad hoc networks for decision
   making. This requires random access on status and description
   of all entities within the overall production network.

4. *Real-time access and processing*: Operative production
   requires real-time control and decision making. Decision
   processes have to consider overall system goals and
   optimization. This requires the processing of comprehensive
   models and accessing network data in real time.

These issues form two general Big Data use cases with
fundamental differences regarding access and processing patterns
and underlying data.

- The first one is *Data Mining*, which handles time-consuming
  data analytics, mining, and prognosis on large amounts of
  passive data. Real-time queries and random access are not
  required. This requires Big Data solutions that support batch
  processing and distributed computing.

- The second one is *Entity Access*, which performs ad hoc queries on entity data from the overall network for operative decision making. This requires Big Data solutions that support real-time queries and random access and may use web services like SOAP or REST.

In the context of this book, we will initially set up the infrastructure and processing for the first use case of data mining that supports Hadoop HDFS and MapReduce processing. Then, we'll examine how to utilize real-time queries in agile analytics.

HADOOP INFRASTRUCTURE: OVERVIEW

- Hadoop Infrastructure is based on an architecture of clusters. A cluster is a configuration of nodes that interact to perform a specific task. In the past these have provided high-performance processing solutions for the aerospace and defense industries.

- Hadoop Distributed File System (HDFS) supports the velocity, variety, volume, and voracity of Big Data as it is laid across the NameNode and DataNodes. We cannot overemphasize the importance of veracity, as this relates to the accuracy of data in predicting business value. A forward-looking business may build a **Smart Data Engine** to analyze massive amounts of data in real time that quickly assesses the value of the customer to build the customer profile. It uses this customer profile to evaluate the potential to provide additional offers to that customer (i.e., **Make the Point-of-Service, the Point-of-Sale**).

- With the advent of commercial IoT, clusters have formed the backbone of important commercial entities such as social media powerhouse Facebook that spreads over thousands of nodes.

- With the advent of the Cloud, it is now possible to have multi-layer clusters such as:

    - Virtual clusters (cluster of virtual machines such as Java Virtual Machine (JVM) that can run on multiple operating systems such as Microsoft Windows, Linux, and Mac). To minimize expenses, install Vagrant or Puppet on Redhat or Ubuntu to set up a cluster of virtual machines.

- Cloud clusters that are massively scalable.

- Real clusters that deploy core application stack such as Amazon S3 platform.

- In a nutshell, Hadoop supports efficient and distributed processing of massive amounts of data by exploiting the latest technologies.

HADOOP INFRASTRUCTURE: DEFINED

Hadoop developers need extremely fast processing platforms to play around with the data in order to find the magical insights concealed in that Big Data. For this, the data residing in the relational database management system (R-DBMS) need to be transferred back and forth to the HDFS. Data experimentation, governance, and culture are now part of the Big Data challenge for organizations. In order to face the challenge of Big Data, a robust and fast Hadoop Infrastructure is needed that capitalizes on the compute, network, and storage technologies. Let us focus on the key features and characteristics of Hadoop Infrastructure.

Hyperconverged Hadoop Infrastructure

There are several options available in the market. For high-quality support of the unique needs of Big Data analytics that powers all data intensive workloads on a centrally managed and highly scalable system, Cisco Unified Computing System (UCS) stands out. The business requirement is to quickly and efficiently deliver out-of-the-box performance while scaling from small to very large as the business and associated Big Data and analytics requirements grow.

Cisco UCS integrates with Cloudera to help organizations realize the value of their structured, semi-structured, and un-structured data. In addition to fast performance, it takes away the headache of platform management and cybersecurity.

Cisco in partnership with NetApp has developed FlexPod, which is a unified computing, storage, and network infrastructure comprised of Cisco UCS servers that deploy massive amounts of shared cache, Cisco UCS Manager, Cisco Nexus family of data switches deploying Q-Logic (Cisco UCS M73KR-Q), and NetApp Fabric Attached Storage (FAS) LUN arrays. In this configuration, the host bus adapters on the UCS servers point to the ports on the data switch, which in turn are fiber attached to the storage LUN (Figure 2.2).

Compute Hardware Components

Given the requirements of Big Data, the computer hardware must live up to the processing requirements of cybersecurity, high performance, scalability, and fault tolerance. In order to meet these requirements, the computer hardware shall be comprised of rack-mounted, scalable blade servers that have multi-core CPUs with a

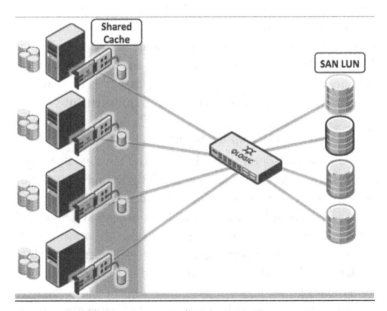

FIGURE 2.2   Hyperconverged infrastructure.

3$^+$ GHz clock rate. These servers must have large shared memory (RAM) in terabytes to be used by data base management systems such as Apache HIVE for the fast retrieval of cached data objects.

For efficient and distributed processing of massive data workloads, load balancers will be deployed that balance load across servers. Additionally, they will use secured socket layer (SSL) encryption and thereby serve as proxy servers to hide the identity of primary web application servers.

For scalable architecture as part of Hadoop Version 2 infrastructure, these servers will be implemented as clustered servers, also called DataNodes or slave servers, that are managed by a synchronous master, also called NameNode or master server.

Network Hardware Components

Big Data requires a fast, fault tolerant, secured, and scalable network. The rack mounted servers and data switches provide the much needed fault tolerance and scalability. From a maintenance standpoint it is more manageable and simple (see Figure 2.3).

The network hardware will be comprised of 100 Gigabits per second bandwidth data switches such as the Cisco Nexus® 7700

Top-of-Rack (TOR)-Network connectivity architecture

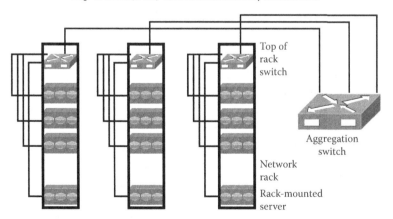

FIGURE 2.3   Network rack architecture. (From excitingip.com.)

F3-Series 12-Port data switch and high speed fiber backbone deploying high speed routers and modems. A simple LAN/WAN topology (see Figure 2.4) shows how the gateway servers, routers, switches, and modems provide the network services. The branch is connected to the central office via the data switch through the Internet or the Cloud. The home office is connected to both the branch and the central office via an Internet modem.

In order to protect the corporate computing resources, the intranet domain and sub-domains are defined for internal corporate use and authorized external users. This is an important cybersecurity measure. For intranet security, high-bandwidth firewalls (see Figure 2.5) are configured to control access to intranet domains and sub-domains. Based on business security requirements, the Name Resolution Policy Table (NRPT) limits network access based on pre-configured firewall ports. Besides the Network firewall, Figure 2.5 also shows the use of host-based firewalls.

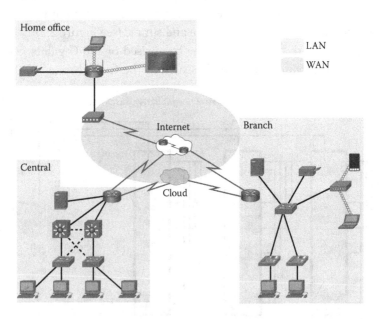

FIGURE 2.4 LAN/WAN topology – Routers, switches, modems. (From ciscopress.com.)

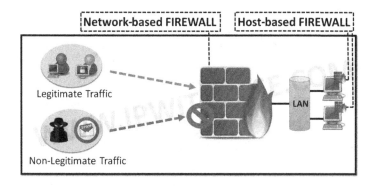

FIGURE 2.5   Network- versus host-based firewalls. (From ipwithease.com.)

Storage Hardware Architecture and Components

In light of the complexity and volume of Big Data, it is important to select a data storage system that provides low latency, high availability, and high performance.

For high-performance and fault-tolerant storage, there are a number of options available in the market. As a major supplier of enterprise storage with over 13% of the market share, NetApp Clustered Storage is in high demand. International Data Corp. reported in 2017: "The growth in storage business has shifted away from the traditional leaders in the business, with NetApp the only traditional vendor to see a significant increase in storage sales." We will therefore review the NetApp Clustered Data ONTAP storage system, as it meets requirements of high-performance and fault-tolerant storage. For simplicity, the architecture of ONE high availability pair, made of of Vserver1 and Vserver2, is presented in Figure 2.6. Please note that the Clustered Data ONTAP storage system can have four or more high availability pairs supporting SAN storage of 23 pitabytes that use cluster interconnect ethernet network bandwidth of 10 Gigabits per second.

To incorporate fault tolerance the high availability pair, as you will observe in the architecture diagram, deploys for each Vserver its own DNS Zone and VLAN. The data network is managed by the Data Vserver. Each Vserver resides on a cluster of multiple nodes

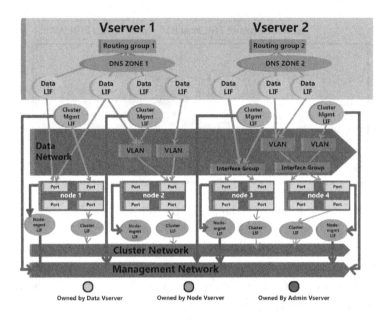

FIGURE 2.6 Clustered data ONTAP storage architecture. (For more information about the basic cluster and Vservers, see the *Clustered Data ONTAP System Administration Guide for Cluster Administrators*.)

which are managed by the Node Vserver. The storage cluster has a management network which is managed by the Admin Vserver.

For high performance, the physical storage made of large disk arrays are striped and carved into storage LUNs. Using fiber channel protocol, NetApp filers deploy high bandwidth data switches to map LUN's fiber channel address to the ports on the data switch, which in turn are mapped to host bus adapters (HBA) on the server backplane using a unique worldwide port name (WWPN).

HADOOP ECO SYSTEM

Hadoop is an open source written in Java. Operations are enabled by Hypervisor or Virtual Machine Computer Software that creates or runs virtual machines. A server on which the hypervisor runs is called either a host machine or a NameNode, and the virtual machines are also called guest machines or DataNodes.

Hadoop provides a framework for scalable, fault-tolerant, and high-performance distributed systems to store and process data across a cluster of commodity servers called nodes. The underlying goals are scalability, reliability, and economics.

Hadoop is comprised of the following:

- A set of operations and interfaces for distributed file systems

- HDFS that facilitates running MapReduce jobs over a cluster of commodity servers

- A Mahout tool to facilitate machine learning

- Processing tools contained in the Cloudera Software Distribution bundle are:

  - HIVE: Uses an Interpretor to transform SQL query to MapReduce code

  - PIG: Scripting language that creates MapReduce code

  - SQOOP: Serves as data exchange between R-DBMS and the HIVE database

  - IMPALA: Uses SQL to access data directly from HDFS

- Hadoop Version 2 Infrastructure that has a master NameNode where the Resource Manager runs and has the meta data about the underlying slave DataNodes

- Hadoop Version 2 Infrastructure that has several DataNodes where the actual fault-tolerant application data resides as well as the Node Manager to keep track of jobs running on DataNode and provides feedback to the Resource Manager that runs on the NameNode

- Hadoop Version 2 Infrastructure can conveniently use fault-tolerant NetApp Clustered Data ONTAP 8.0 that provides the operational framework of Vserver that manages multiple sub-servient DataNodes using Data Logical Interfaces (see Figure 2.6)

HADOOP: JVM FRAMEWORK

The Java Virtual Machine (JVM) enables a computer to run Java programs as well as programs not written in Java. The Java Compile Time Environment compiles Java source code into the Byte code. The Java Run Time Environment interprets the Byte code and produces platform specific executable assignments (Figure 2.7).

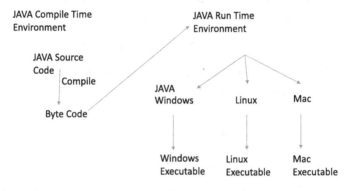

FIGURE 2.7   Hadoop JVM framework.

HADOOP DISTRIBUTED FILE PROCESSING

Hadoop Version 2 uses 5 daemon services, out of which there are 3 NameNode services running on the Master Node. These services are also called master services. Additionally, there are 2 DataNode services running on the Slave Node. These services are also called slave services.

The NameNode services are NameNode, Resource Manager, and Secondary NameNode. The DataNode services are DataNode and Task Tracker. These daemon services manage the data processing across the cluster of NameNode and distributed DataNodes.

- HDFS supports the velocity, variety, volume, and veracity of Big Data. A thorough understanding of how this data is laid out and managed is of paramount importance. The metadata and actual data reside on specific directories on the HDFS server.

- An example of 1 NameNode directory (also called Master Node that stores Metadata) and 10 DataNode directories (also called slave nodes that store actual application data) are given below:

- Metadata:
  /home/osboxes/lab/hdfs/namenodep

- Actual Data:
  /home/osboxes/lab/hdfs/datan1, /home/osboxes/lab/hdfs/datan2
  /home/osboxes/lab/hdfs/datan3, /home/osboxes/lab/hdfs/datan4
  /home/osboxes/lab/hdfs/datan5, /home/osboxes/lab/hdfs/datan6
  /home/osboxes/lab/hdfs/datan7, /home/osboxes/lab/hdfs/datan8
  /home/osboxes/lab/hdfs/datan9, /home/osboxes/lab/hdfs/datan10

- The DataNode directories previously shown on the HDFS server use symbolic links to point to the directories on slave nodes where the application data resides. Again, metadata about files on HDFS are stored and managed on NameNode. This includes information like permissions and ownership of such files, location of various blocks of that file on DataNodes, etc.

TUTORIAL: HADOOP DISTRIBUTED FILE SYSTEM COMMANDS

HDFS uses flavors of Linux such as Cloudera, Ubuntu, or Hortonworks. A thorough understanding of HDFS commands is important, as we need to perform file manipulations on the HDFS server. This tutorial will walk through the important and most commonly used commands.

- Simple Rule: Prefix Linux commands with "hadoop fs –"

  - List all files under present working directory:
    ```
    hadoop fs -ls
    ```

- Create new directory under root directory:
  ```
  hadoop fs -mkdir /new-directory
  ```

- Create new directory under present working directory:
  ```
  hadoop fs -mkdir ./new-directory
  ```

- Find file sizes under new directory:
  ```
  hadoop fs -du -s /new-directory
  ```

- Count the number of directories under the /etc directory:
  ```
  hadoop fs -count /etc
  ```

Remove "sample" file from HDFS directory:
```
hadoop fs -rm /hdfs/cloudera/sample
System Response: Deleted Sample
```

Remove "bigdata" directory from HDFS directory:
```
hadoop fs -rm -r /hdfs/cloudera/bigdata
System Response: Deleted bigdata
```

Copy file from Local File System to HDFS
The syntax is:

```
hadoop fs -copyFromLocal <local file> URI
```

where URI is a string of characters used to identify a resource over the network

Example:
```
hadoop  fs  -copyFromLocal  /home/cloudera/
hadooptraining /hdfs/cloudera
```

Where local file = /home/cloudera/hadooptraining and URI = /hdfs/cloudera

Check if the file copy to URI worked:
```
hadoop fs -ls /hdfs/cloudera/hadooptraining
```

Copy complete directory from Local File System to HDFS
The syntax is:

```
hadoop fs -put <local directory> <hdfs directory>
```

Example:
```
hadoop fs -put /home/cloudera/bigdata /hdfs/
cloudera
```

Where local directory = /home/cloudera and
hdfs directory = /hdfs/cloudera

Check if 'bigdata' directory was copied:
```
hadoop fs -ls /hdfs/cloudera
```

Copy complete directory from HDFS to Local File System
The syntax is:

```
hadoop fs -get -crc <HDFS directory> <local
directory>
```

Example:
```
hadoop fs -get -crc /hdfs/cloudera/bigdata
/home/cloudera
```

Where hdfs directory = /hdfs/cloudera and local directory =
/home/cloudera

Check if 'bigdata' directory was copied:
```
hadoop fs -ls /home/cloudera
```

TUTORIAL: DISTRIBUTION OF INPUT DATA
IN HDFS ACROSS DATA NODES

We have already reviewed the HDFS commands that will be used
to perform file manipulation on the DataNode (Figure 2.8). In
order to support fast and efficient parallel processing and built-in

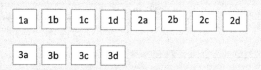

FIGURE 2.8   Input data distribution across 12 data nodes.

fault tolerance provided by HDFS, the input data is split into "n" partitions and replicated based on the HDFS Replication Factor.

Assumption:

Large Input data: sample.txt

Number of partitions = 4 (a,b,c,d)

HDFS Replication Factor = 3 (fault tolerance)

sample.txt
a
b
c
d

Note: MapReduce runs in parallel on many nodes but <u>runs on each node separately</u>.

MapReduce SOFTWARE

- MapReduce is the distributed data processing model that runs on a large cluster of servers.

- It uses a parallel algorithm that allows linear scaling and runs in batch job mode. It suites business intelligence applications that run on the WORM paradigm. No wonder, Informatica Big Data Management tool uses ETL connector for HIVE

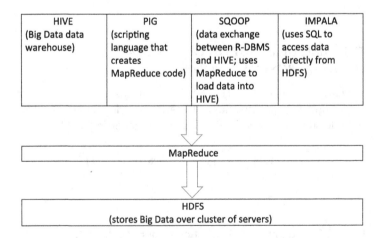

HIVE (Big Data data warehouse)	PIG (scripting language that creates MapReduce code)	SQOOP (data exchange between R-DBMS and HIVE; uses MapReduce to load data into HIVE)	IMPALA (uses SQL to access data directly from HDFS)

MapReduce

HDFS
(stores Big Data over cluster of servers)

FIGURE 2.9 Cloudera software distribution bundle.

that runs MapReduce to deliver the industry's first and most comprehensive solution to natively ingest, integrate, cleanse, govern, and secure Big Data workloads on Hadoop platforms.

- MapReduce software is included in the Cloudera distribution package, which has a number of other Hadoop tools that are designed to run on clustered nodes under the HDFS framework (Figure 2.9).

MapReduce SOFTWARE INSTALLATION

- MapReduce is a programming model and an associated implementation for processing and generating Big Data sets with a parallel, distributed algorithm that runs on a cluster of nodes.

- Under the Oracle VM Virtual Box Manager, install Cloudera in Oracle VM Virtual Box. MapReduce is installed as part of the Cloudera software bundle.

- Please connect to the URL to: https://download.virtualbox. org/virtualbox/5.2.8/;.
  Then select from the list: VirtualBox-5.2.8-121009-Win.exe

- The summary of minimal system requirements are as follows:
  - 64 bit Windows Operating System
  - VM Box/Player 4.x and higher
  - Host Operating System must have at least 8 GB memory
  - VM needs at least 4 GB RAM

Note: <u>Usage of MapReduce in business intelligence</u>—In terms of processing, business intelligence runs on the WORM paradigm, which is consistent with MapReduce processing. Therefore, the Informatica Big Data Management tool uses ETL Connector for **HIVE** that runs **MapReduce** to deliver the industry's first and most comprehensive solution to natively ingest, integrate, clean, govern, and secure Big Data workloads on the Hadoop platforms.

MAPREDUCE PROCESSING

- By now we know that MapReduce processing uses Apache Hadoop that stores and processes data in a distributed fashion. In Hadoop Version 2, the NameNode and Resource Manager daemons are master daemons, whereas the DataNode and Node Manager daemons are slave daemons. This framework of NameNode and underlying DataNodes takes care of scheduling tasks, monitoring them, and re-executing the failed tasks.

- Cloudera YARN has a master/worker architecture (see Figure 2.10); the master (the Resource Manager running on NameNode) manages the resources for the workers (the Node Manager running on DataNodes). Furthermore, the Resource Manager handles all client interactions (see Figure 2.10).

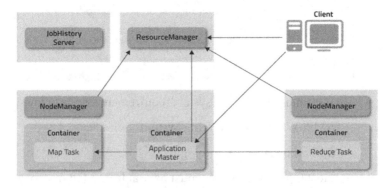

FIGURE 2.10   YARN architecture. (From blog.cloudera.com.)

As we have observed in the earlier tutorial, a MapReduce *job* usually splits the input dataset into independent chunks which are processed by the *map tasks* in a completely parallel manner. The framework sorts the outputs of the maps, which are then input to the *reduce tasks*. Typically, both the input and the output of the job are stored in a file system.

- The "MapReduce System" (also called "infrastructure" or "framework") orchestrates the processing by marshalling the distributed nodes, running the various tasks in parallel, managing all communications and data transfers between the various parts of the system, and providing for redundancy and fault tolerance as defined by the Replication Factor in HDFS configuration.

- What is a MapReduce program? A MapReduce program is composed of a mapper (Java class), which performs filtering and sorting (such as sorting students by first name into queues, one queue for each name), and a reducer (Java class), which performs a summary operation (such as counting the number of students in each queue, yielding name frequencies et cetera).

CONCEPTUAL TUTORIAL: MapReduce PROCESSING

Note: Although there are other software solutions as offered by Cassandra, a common algorithm is MapReduce, which is tuned for specific use cases. A representative software solution for this principle is Hadoop HDFS with MapReduce. In summary, this is the Big Data solution for Use Case that supports batch processing and distributed computing, such as Hadoop HDFS with MapReduce.

- *Mapper Class*
  - Maps input into key/value pairs which in turn are mapped to a set of intermediate key/value pairs.

- *Shuffler Class*

  - Exchanges intermediate key/value pairs to where they are required by the reducers.

  This process is called shuffling.

  For example, after the mapping and shuffling of Walmart stores, we have input key/value pairs in the Mappers as follows:

M_1	M_2	M_3	M_4	M_5	M_6	M_7	M_8
Los Angeles/	New York/	San Jose/	Chicago/	Houston/	Miami/	Princeton/	Minneapolis/
100	110	50	80	70	75	75	70

- *Reducer Class*

  - Reduces a set of intermediate values which share just one key. All of the intermediate values for this key are presented to the reducer. This Java class generates "sorted key value sets," where each set belongs to single key value.
  For example after reduction, we have the following values in the reducers:

R_1 (West)	R_2 (East)	R_3 (South)	R_4 (North)
150	185	145	150

- *Driver Class*

  - Configures and runs Mapper, Shuffler, and Reducer classes.

TUTORIAL: PSEUDO CODE FOR MapReduce JAVA CLASSES

The public Java class "emit" extends Java language object. This class emits generated code for the parser. The value_out is generated by parsing the input string and provides the pair of "key, value."

- Given: address, zip, city, house_value. Calculate the average house value for each zip code.

- The pseudo code is as follows:

```
inpt = load 'data.txt' as (address:chararray,
zip:chararray, city:chararray, house _
value:long); grp = group inpt by zip;
average = foreach grp generate FLATTEN(group)
as (zip), AVG(inpt.house _ value) as average _
price; dump average;
MAPPER(record): zip _ code _ key = record['zip'];
value = {1, record['house _ value']};
emit(zip _ code _ key, value);
SHUFFLER(zip _ code _ key, value _ list):
record _ num = 0;
value _ sum = 0;
foreach (value : value _ list)
{ record _ num += value[0];
value _ sum += value[1]; }
value _ out = {record _ num, value _ sum};
emit(zip _ code _ key, value _ out);
REDUCER(zip _ code _ key, value _ list):
record _ num = 0;
value _ sum = 0;
foreach (value : value _ list)
{ record _ num += value[0];
value _ sum += value[1]; }
avg = value _ sum / record _ num;
emit(zip _ code _ key, avg);
```

CHAPTER 3

Big Data Use Cases

OVERVIEW

Now that we have scratched the tip of the iceberg that is Big Data, let us see how it is being applied in real life. We will briefly review three areas of application that are major consumers of Big Data: health, manufacturing, and insurance.

BIG DATA USE CASE: HEALTH

By <u>one conservative estimate</u>, applying Big Data analytics on a health system-wide basis could reduce health care spending in the United States by a staggering $300–$450 billion annually.

Health care providers have made strides in collecting and sharing massive amounts of data in electronic health records and health information exchanges. The semi-structured and un-structured data are stored in Big Data databases such as HIVE. These are electronic health records such as doctor transcripts, laboratory diagnostics, and nurse observations, which are passed through the MapReduce process.

In the aforementioned case (see Figure 3.1),[5] the click-stream data related to medical symptoms such as schizophrenia, cardiac, pulmonary, oncology, and diabetic conditions are captured from the IoT.

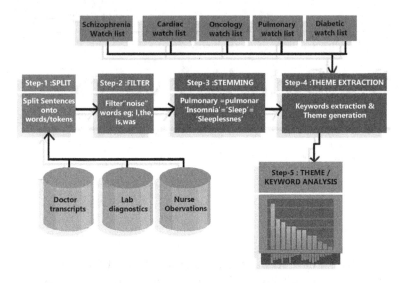

FIGURE 3.1   Big Data use case – health. (From blog.flutura.com.)

What had been lacking is the analytics piece of the equation; the missing link to making sense of all this and other data. As shown in Figure 3.1, through a process of keyword extraction, a theme is generated for analytics. Until recently, these efforts had little impact on costs or on patient outcomes for that matter. Moreover, there is every reason to believe that patient outcomes will improve as well, perhaps substantially.

We cannot overemphasize the use of Hadoop and Big Data analytics in health care. It is worth noting that in the health care environment, more than three-quarters of the data available for use is un-structured data. It comes from an ever-growing list of sources, including thousands of devices and sensors, medical staff notes, lab tests, imaging reports, and many outside sources of medical information. This is data that is the bread and butter for the Hadoop platform. It isn't just the un-structured nature of most health care data that matches up well with Hadoop. It is also the sheer enormity of the data volumes from these and other sources, which would easily overwhelm traditional analytics platforms.

Hadoop is capable of acquiring and storing gigantic masses of any kind of data.

As we learnt earlier, MapReduce runs in parallel on many inexpensive nodes but <u>runs on each node separately</u>. In Hadoop Version 2, Cloudera YARN (see Figure 2.10) manages all tasks running on the subservient DataNodes.

BIG DATA USE CASE: MANUFACTURING

A Big Data use case provides a focus for analytics, providing parameters for the types of data that can be of value and determining how to model that data using Hadoop analytics. For example, it plays a critical role in answering questions such as "What is the accuracy of next run failure?" or "What is the accuracy in quality check?" (see Figure 3.2). The following example is a Big Data use case in the manufacturing industry.[3]

Under Industry 4.0, Big Data analytics is useful in predictive manufacturing and is a major theme for industrial technology development. To assist manufacturers in maintaining a competitive edge in operational management control and in improving their

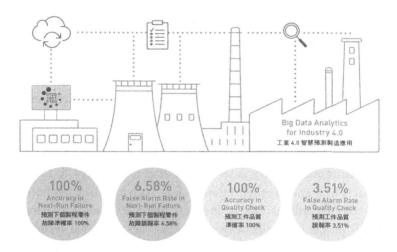

FIGURE 3.2 Big Data analytics for Industry 4.0. (From itri.org.tw.)

production efficiency and yield rates, the International Technology Research Institute has developed a Big Data analytics solution with integrated ensemble learning capability.

An advanced machine learning algorithm analyzes process data collected from production systems to provide early warning for anomalies and system failures and to predict product quality. An accuracy of up to 100% and false alarm rates of less than 6.58% have been achieved in the prediction of the next-run failure of components along the line. The algorithm also achieves 100% accuracy and 3.51% false alarm rate in predicting the quality (Go/No Go) of the workpiece next in line. This intelligent solution for the manufacturing sector can nurture information service providers' capacities in Big Data analytics. It is also suitable for the epitaxial process and a wide range of semi-conductor and machining applications.

The digital revolution has transformed the manufacturing industry. Manufacturers are now finding new ways to harness all the data they generate to improve operational efficiency, streamline business processes, and uncover valuable insights that will drive profits and growth.

As we see in Figure 3.2, to be able to predict next-run failure with 100% accuracy gives an immense advantage to predict equipment failure which can form the basis of Predictive Machine Tool Maintenance.

Companies must integrate data coming in different formats, look for signals that point to adverse machine productivity, and use this data to optimize machine tool maintenance.

BIG DATA USE CASE: INSURANCE

The insurance industry is taking the lead in this regard. Many insurers now analyze their internal data, such as call center notes and voice recordings, alongside social media data and third party details on people's bills, wages, bankruptcies, criminal records, and address changes to gain insight into potentially fraudulent claims.

For example, while a claimant may declare their car was damaged by flooding, their social media feed may indicate weather conditions were sunny on the day of the supposed incident. Insurers can supplement this data with text analytics technology that can detect minor discrepancies hidden in a claimant's case report. Fraudsters tend to alter their story over time, making this a powerful tool in detecting criminal activity.

The insurance sector has traditionally analyzed fraud data in silos and largely ignored un-structured data points, but this is changing. According to Morgan Stanley, a more advanced analytics approach helps insurers improve fraud detection rates by 30%.

In addition to cost-savings, advanced analytics is helping businesses improve the customer experience and protect their brand reputation too. For insurers, fraud-related losses are not only detrimental to their finances, but can lead to price increases for customers and lengthen review times for legitimate claims. Honest customers have little patience for this, so the ability to keep fraud to a minimum is crucial to keep turnover down.

This data requires development of 3-D dashboards, which require the integration of different transaction data with additional information such as interaction events or sequence of events in real time and customer behavior (customer's entire online journey) as captured from the click-stream data. For pre-emptive fraud prevention, it is important to be able to capture potential fraud patterns, which can then be used advantageously over and over again. These are some of the challenges for the insurance industry.

CHAPTER 4

Big Data Migration

OVERVIEW

Apache SQOOP stands out in the Big Data world when we talk about data migration. It was created in 2009 by Aaron Kimball as a means of moving data between SQL databases and Hadoop. It provided a generic implementation for moving data. It also provided a framework for implementing database specific optimized connectors.

Apache SQOOP is a powerful data exchange between data stores such as R-DBMS and Enterprise Data Warehouse on the one hand and HIVE and HBase on the other. In other words, <u>Apache SQOOP supports 2-way traffic between R-DBMS and Hadoop</u>.

R-DBMS	Hadoop
Teradata	HIVE
Oracle	HBase
Netezza	
MySQL	
Postgres	

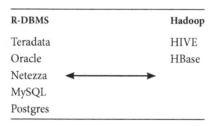

- Apache SQOOP is a tool designed for efficiently transferring bulk data between Apache Hadoop and external data stores such as relational databases and enterprise data warehouses.

- SQOOP is used to import data from external datastores into HDFS or related Hadoop Eco systems like HIVE and HBase. Similarly, SQOOP can also be used to extract data from Hadoop or its eco systems and export it to external datastores such as relational databases and enterprise data warehouses. SQOOP works with relational databases such as Teradata, Netezza, Oracle, MySQL, Postgres, etc.

- Why is Apache SQOOP used?

- For Hadoop developers, the interesting work starts after data is loaded into HDFS. Developers play around with the data in order to find the magical insights concealed in that Big Data. For this, the data residing in the relational database management systems need to be transferred to HDFS, played around with, and might need to be transferred back to relational database management systems. In the reality of the Big Data world, developers feel the transferring of data back and forth between relational and Hadoop DB database systems and HDFS is required. Developers can always write custom scripts to transfer.

- Developers need to access R-DBMS to make sense of Hadoop data. They want to use Hadoop to analyze R-DBMS data. We migrate old R-DBMS data to Hadoop/HDFS platforms such as HIVE. The data warehouse constructs in HIVE are accessible via BI connectors from the Tableau BI tool. This facilitates complex data analytics as in 3-D dashboards.

- Apache SQOOP provides a command line interface, which can be scripted for repeat operations. As we will observe in the tutorial, we only need to provide basic information such as source, destination, network connection string, and database authentication.

- Apache SQOOP automates most of the process and depends on the database to describe the schema of the data to be imported. Apache SQOOP uses MapReduce framework to import and export the data, which provides parallel mechanisms as well as fault tolerances. Apache SQOOP makes a developer's life easy by providing command line interface. Developers just need to provide basic information details in the Apache SQOOP command, and it takes care of the remaining parts.

- Apache SQOOP provides many salient features like full load, incremental load, parallel import/export, import results of SQL query, connectors for all major R-DBMSs, and load data directly into HIVE/Hbase.

- Apache SQOOP is robust, has great community support and contributions, and is widely used in most of the Big Data companies to transfer data between relational databases and Hadoop.

CHALLENGES IN MIGRATING ORACLE DATA USING SQOOP

In MapReduce processing, SQOOP uses primary key ranges to divide up data between mappers. However, the deletes hit older key values harder, making key ranges unbalanced. Balanced key ranges across index blocks will require reverse key indexes. Reverse indexes have become particularly important in high-volume transaction processing systems because they reduce contention for index blocks. Take the Oracle sequence number 24538, the next number is 24539 and so on, all concentrated on the same index block that will cause IO contention. In the reverse index, these numbers will be 83542 and 93542, which will spread farther apart on the index blocks causing very little IO contention.

WHERE IS SQOOP USED?

- Relational database systems are widely used to interact with the traditional business applications. So, relational database systems have become one of the sources that generate Big Data.

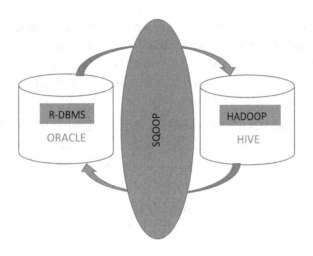

FIGURE 4.1   Data exchange – SQOOP.

- As we are dealing with Big Data, Hadoop stores and processes the Big Data using different processing frameworks like MapReduce, Cassandra, and PIG and storage frameworks like HDFS, HIVE, and HBase to achieve the benefits of distributed computing and distributed storage. In order to store and analyze the Big Data from relational databases, data need to be transferred between database systems and HDFS. Here, SQOOP comes into picture, acting like an intermediate layer between Hadoop and relational database systems. You can import data and export data between relational database systems and Hadoop and its eco systems directly using SQOOP (Figure 4.1).

SQOOP COMMANDS

- **SQOOP-Import Generic Syntax:**
  ```
  $ sqoop import (generic args) (import args)
  ```
- **Importing a Table into HDFS**
  ```
  $ sqoop import --connect --table --username \
  -password --target-dir
  ```

- **Importing Selected Data from Table**
  ```
  $ sqoop import --connect --table --username \
  --password --columns -where clause
  ```

- **Importing Data from Query**
  ```
  $ sqoop import --connect --table --username \
  --password --query
  ```

- **Importing Data into HIVE**
  ```
  $ sqoop import --connect --table --username \
  --password --hive-import --hive-table
  ```

HIVE ARGUMENTS USED BY SQOOP

Argument	Description
--hive-home	Override $HIVE_HOME path
--hive-import	Import tables into HIVE
--hive-overwrite	Overwrites existing HIVE table data
--create-hive-table	Creates HIVE table and fails if that table already exists
--hive-table	Sets the HIVE table name to import
--hive-drop-import-delims	Drops delimiters like\n, \r, and \01 from string fields
--hive-delims-replacement	Replaces delimiters like \n, \r, and \01 from string fields with user defined delimiters
--hive-partition-key	Sets the HIVE partition key
--hive-partition-value	Sets the HIVE partition value
--map-column-hive	Overrides default mapping from SQL type datatypes to HIVE datatypes

TUTORIAL: APACHE SQOOP INSTALLATION

Under the Oracle VM Virtual Box Manager, install Cloudera in Oracle VM Virtual Box. SQOOP is installed as part of the Cloudera software bundle on the Hadoop server. All interactive commands are typed at UNIX prompt ($).

1. Change directory to the SQOOP directory created by the Cloudera software bundle:

   ```
   $ hadoop fs -cd /usr/bin/sqoop
   ```

2. Unzip the tar file:
   ```
   $ hadoop fs -sudo tar -zxvf \
   sqoop-1.4.4.bin_hadoop1.0.0.tar.gz
   ```

3. Create a directory SQOOP under /usr/lib
   ```
   $hadoop fs -sudo mkdir /usr/lib/sqoop
   ```

4. Move sqoop-1.4.4.bin hadoop1.0.0 to /usr/lib/sqoop
   ```
   $ hadoop fs -sudo mv \
   sqoop-1.4.4.bin-hadoop1.0.0 /usr/lib/sqoop/.
   ```

5. Go to the /usr/lib/sqoop directory and execute
   sqoop-1.4.4.bin_hadoop-1.0.0
   ```
   $ hadoop fs -sudo ./ \
   sqoop-1.4.4.bin_hadoop-1.0.0
   ```

6. Go to root directory using cd command
   ```
   $ hadoop fs -sudo cd /
   ```

7. Open .bashrc file using
   ```
   $ hadoop fs -sudo gedit ./.bashrc
   ```

8. Add the following lines
   ```
   $ hadoop fs -export SQOOP_HOME=/usr/lib/sqoop
   $ hadoop fs -export PATH=$PATH:$SQOOP_HOME/bin
   ```

9. To check if the SQOOP has been installed successfully type the command
   ```
   $ sqoop version
   ```

APACHE SQOOP ARCHITECTURE

In cases where data volume is high, transformations are slowing down the R-DBMS and face bottlenecks on query performance. Transformations are much better suited for a batch processing system like Hadoop, which offers the agility to work with any data type and are very scalable. SQOOP is the facilitator of data transfer from enterprise data warehouse, document based systems, and R-DBMS to HDFS/HIVE. SQOOP generates the

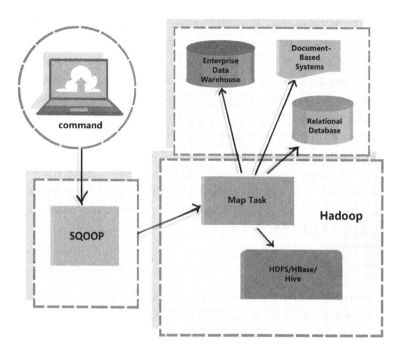

FIGURE 4.2   SQOOP architecture. (From packtpub.com)

MapReduce code to migrate data to either HDFS directory or HIVE tables (Figure 4.2).

APACHE SQOOP COMMAND LINE INTERFACE

SQOOP provides a command line interface to the end users. SQOOP can also be accessed using Java APIs. SQOOP command submitted by the end user is parsed by SQOOP and launches Hadoop Map, with its only job being to import or export data because the reduce phase is required only when aggregations are needed. SQOOP just imports and exports the data; it does not do any aggregations.

SQOOP parses the arguments provided in the command line and prepares the map job. The map job launches multiple mappers that depend on the number defined by user in the command line.

For the SQOOP import, each mapper task will be assigned with the part of data to be imported based on the key defined in the command line. SQOOP distributes the input data among the mappers equally to get high performance. Then, each mapper creates a connection with the database using the Java database connectivity (jdbc) connect string and fetches the part of data assigned by SQOOP and writes it into HDFS, Hive, or HBase based on the option provided in the command line.

HIVE Data Warehouse supports Star Schema. Since there is one-to-many 1:N cardinality between the dimension tables and the FACT table, we need to first migrate all dimension tables and then migrate the FACT table.

TUTORIAL: USE OF SQOOP TO MIGRATE DATA FROM ORACLE TO HDFS DIRECTORY AND HIVE

The HIVE database can be used as a data warehouse for the following reasons. It can therefore be effectively used as a repository of Big Data to perform data analytics.

- HIVE database supports star schema.
- HIVE database supports slow changing dimensions.
- HIVE database supports dimension hierarchy that can be used for data roll-ups and drill-drowns.

As a tutorial, we will migrate the star schema from Oracle data warehouse to HDFS directory as well as the HIVE database. The star schema is comprised of the Shipment FACT table and it's DIMENSION table. Since there is one-to-many cardinality between the DIMENSION table and FACT table, we will first migrate all DIMENSION tables and finally migrate the FACT table.

- Migrate SHIPMENT **FACT** table in the Data Warehouse Oracle 11g database. This **FACT** table is in a star schema with **DIMENSIONs**, PRODUCT, CURRENCY, CALENDAR, CUSTOMER, and SALES_ORDER.

Assumptions:

- IP address of Oracle DB server is 192.168.197.1
- Oracle D.B Listener is listening on Port 1521
- Oracle SID is "dwh11g"
- SQOOP "import" executable exists on the HDFS server in /usr/bin directory
- Target directory on HDFS server, /home/cloudera/bigdata
- The system username has the "select" privilege on all DIMENSION tables and the FACT table.
- We will look into two ways to migrate data from Oracle database to HDFS:
  - Import to a target directory on HDFS server
  - Import to HIVE database running on HDFS server

1. Import DIMENSIONs and FACT tables to a target directory on HDFS server

Set up SQOOP_BIN variable

```
$hadoop fs -export SQOOP_BIN=/usr/lib/sqoop/bin

$SQOOP_BIN import  --connect
jdbc:oracle:thin:system/ \
system@192.168.197.1:1521:dwh11g--username
SYSTEM -password welcome --table system.PRODUCT
target-dir / home/cloudera/bigdata -m 1

$SQOOP_BIN import  --connect
jdbc:oracle:thin:system/ \
system@192.168.197.1:1521:dwh11g--username
SYSTEM -password welcome --table system.CURRENCY
target-dir / home/cloudera/bigdata -m 1

$SQOOP_BIN import  --connect
jdbc:oracle:thin:system/ \
system@192.168.197.1:1521:dwh11g--username
SYSTEM -password welcome --table system.CALENDAR
target-dir / home/cloudera/bigdata -m 1

$SQOOP_BIN import  --connect
jdbc:oracle:thin:system/ \
```

```
system@192.168.197.1:1521:dwh11g--username
SYSTEM -password welcome --table system.CUSTOMER
target-dir / home/cloudera/bigdata -m 1

$SQOOP_BIN import  --connect
jdbc:oracle:thin:system/ \
system@192.168.197.1:1521:dwh11g--username
SYSTEM -password welcome --table system.SALES_
ORDER target-dir \ home/cloudera/bigdata -m 1

$SQOOP_BIN import  --connect
jdbc:oracle:thin:system/ \ system@192.168.197.1
:1521:dwh11g --username
SYSTEM -password welcome --table system.SHIPMENT
target-dir / home/cloudera/bigdata -m 1
```

2. Import DIMENSIONs and FACT tables to HIVE database running on HDFS server

```
$SQOOP_24 BIN import  --connect
jdbc:oracle:thin:system/ system@192.168.197.1:
1521:dwh11g --username SYSTEM -password welcome
--table system.PRODUCT -hive-import -hive-table

$SQOOP_BIN import  --connect
jdbc:oracle:thin:system/ system@192.168.197.1:
1521:dwh11g --username SYSTEM -password welcome
--table system.CURRENCY -hive-import -hive-table

$SQOOP_BIN import  --connect
jdbc:oracle:thin:system/ system@192.168.197.1:
1521:dwh11g --username SYSTEM -password welcome
--table system.CALENDAR -hive-import -hive-table

$SQOOP_BIN import  --connect
jdbc:oracle:thin:system/ system@192.168.197.1:
1521:dwh11g --username SYSTEM -password welcome
--table system.CUSTOMER -hive-import -hive-table

$SQOOP_BIN import  --connect
jdbc:oracle:thin:system/ system@192.168.197.1:
1521:dwh11g --username SYSTEM -password welcome
--table system.SALES_ORDER -hive-import
-hive-table

$SQOOP_BIN import  --connect
jdbc:oracle:thin:system/ system@192.168.197.1:
1521:dwh11g --username SYSTEM -password welcome
--table system.SHIPMENT -hive-import -hive-table
```

CHAPTER 5

Big Data Ingestion, Integration, and Management

OVERVIEW

In order to extract the benefits of Big Data, we understand that we need to go back and forth between legacy R-DBMS and Hadoop data such as HIVE. We want to use Hadoop to analyze R-DBMS data. We feed legacy R-DBMS data to the Hadoop/HIVE Data Warehouse. For data analytics, we use Tableau BI connectors to access the HIVE Data Warehouse/Data Mart.

In Big Data processing, the most common architecture pattern followed is the hybrid model that supports both schools of thought, that is, *Data Mining*, which handles time-consuming data processing, mining, and prognosis on large amounts of passive data, and *agile analytics*, which supports real-time queries and random access and bypasses the time-consuming batch processing. This hybrid model will require the following tools: Informatica Big Data Management that takes care of the ETL, IMPALA that uses SQL to access data directly from HIVE

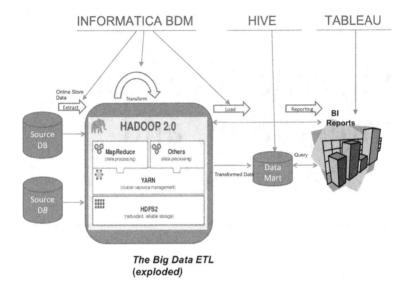

FIGURE 5.1   Hybrid Big Data processing model.

and validates with R-DBMS Query output, HIVE that is used as the Data Mart for reporting, and Tableau that is used as the Data Visualization tool for agile analytics (see Figure 5.1). In this model, the Data Mart can use their existing SQLs or can replace the R-DBMS with NoSQL database(s) like Mongo DB, Cassandra, and so on. Informatica Big Data Management in conjunction with Hadoop can perform transformation much more effectively than R-DBMS. Besides the performance benefits, it is also very fault tolerant and elastic.

INFORMATICA: MATURE AND COMPREHENSIVE BIG DATA SOLUTION

Informatica Big Data Management supports all types of Big Data processing.[7]

1. HIVE on MapReduce

2. HIVE on Tez

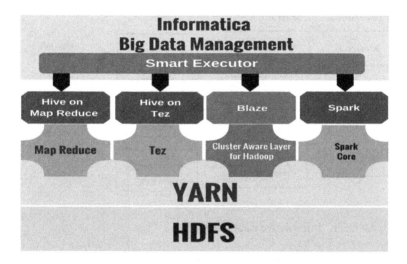

FIGURE 5.2   Informatica support for Big Data processing.[7] (From *BISP Trainings: Live Training on Business Intelligence Tools.* http://bisptrainings.com/, ***BISP Trainings*** is an online training provider with the most powerful learning ... Live Training on Business Intelligence Tools.)

3. Blaze

4. Spark

All of the aforementioned Big Data processing methods use Cloudera-YARN for cluster management and HDFS for storage (see Figure 5.2).

Companies that are turning petabytes into profit have realized that Big Data Management is the foundation for successful Big Data projects. Think about the Data Lakes comprised of structured, semi-structured, and un-structured data sources on the one hand, and Big Data warehouse and visualization tools on the other. Who will build the bridge? That's where Informatica Big Data Management steps in. Even before the inception of Big Data, Informatica was widely acclaimed to provide best-of-breed and high-quality data integration services across multiple source systems (see Figure 5.3).

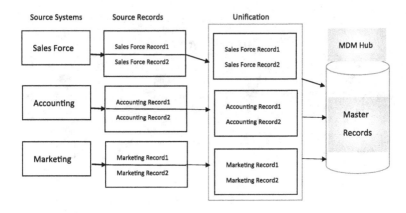

FIGURE 5.3   Informatica data integration.

INFORMATICA DATA INTEGRATION

The Informatica Master Data Management (MDM) hub's Data Steward provides the filters and routers that perform the following tasks:

1. Performs data cleansing by removing duplicate data. It ensures consistent data naming standards and use of data attributes that share a consistent meaning across all source systems.

2. Performs data discovery of missing data across multiple source systems and consequently performs data matching and data merging to come up with best-of-breed integrated data.

In order to maintain a high level of data quality, Informatica uses a complex processing model (see Figure 5.4) to deal effectively with challenges such as:

- Data scattered across systems
  - Difficult to get all data for single entity
  - Fragmented data
  - Spaghetti ETL to integrate
  - Duplicate data

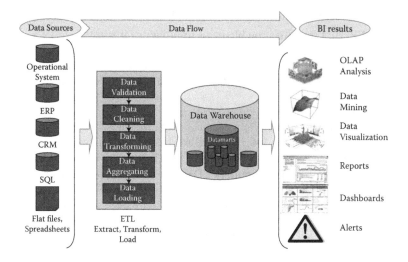

FIGURE 5.4   Informatica data flow.

- Overlapping data
  - Conflicting data
  - Differing update frequencies
  - Spaghetti ETL synchronization

In conclusion, the Informatica Big Data Management tool delivers the industry's first and most comprehensive solution to natively ingest, integrate, clean, govern, and secure Big Data workloads in Hadoop. This data management tool is widely used in majority of Big Data projects that fall into one of two broad categories:

i. Storage driven

ii. Application driven

Figure 5.4 shows the Informatica ETL Process Flow. It visually shows how the source system data in On-Line Transaction Processing (OLTP) systems undergo the Validation, Cleaning, Transforming, and Aggregating processes before getting loaded into the Data Warehouse for On-Line Analytical Processing (OLAP) that provides the business intelligence insights.[8]

TUTORIAL: INFORMATICA BDM INSTALLATION

OVERVIEW

When we install Big Data Management, we install Informatica binaries on the Hadoop cluster. We download an installation package based on the distribution in the Hadoop environment. In our case, we will use **Cloudera CDH**. The following table lists the Hadoop distributions and the associated package types that we use to install Big Data Management.

Hadoop Distribution	Installation Package Description
Amazon EMR	The tar.gz file includes an RPM package and the binary files that you need to run the Big Data Management installation.
Azure HDInsight	The tar.gz file includes a Debian package and the binary files that you need to run the Big Data Management installation.
Cloudera CDH	The parcel.tar file includes a Cloudera parcel package and the binary files that you need to run the Big Data Management installation.
Hortonworks HDP	The archive file includes Big Data Management libraries that are compatible with Ambari stack installation.
IBM BigInsights	The tar.gz file includes an RPM package and the binary files that you need to run the Big Data Management installation.

We will Install Informatica BDM in a Hadoop Cluster Environment.[9]

1. Extract the Big Data Management tar.gz file to a machine on the Hadoop cluster.

2. Install Big Data Management by running the installation shell script in a Linux environment. You can install Big Data Management from the primary NameNode or from any machine using the HadoopDataNodes file.

Add the IP addresses or machine host names, one for each line, for each of the nodes in the Hadoop cluster in the Hadoop DataNodes file. During the Big Data Management installation, the installation shell script picks up all of the nodes from the HadoopDataNodes file and copies the Big Data Management binary files to the /<BigDataManagementInstallationDirectory>/ Informatica directory on each of the nodes.

TUTORIAL: PRE-INSTALLATION TASKS

Install and Configure the Informatica Domain and Clients

Before you install Big Data Management, install and configure the Informatica domain and clients. Run the Informatica services installation to configure the Informatica domain and create the Informatica services.[9] Run the Informatica client installation to install the Informatica client tools.

As our Big Data Repository is HIVE, we will only install and configure PowerExchange Adapter for HIVE.

Install and Configure PowerExchange Adapter

PowerExchange for Hive

Install and Configure Data Replication

To migrate data with minimal downtime and perform auditing and operational reporting functions, install and configure Data Replication. For information, see the Informatica Data Replication User Guide.

Pre-Installation Tasks on Master Node (NameNode)

Verify that Hadoop is installed with HDFS and MapReduce.[9] The Hadoop installation should include a HIVE data warehouse that is configured to use a MySQL database as the Metastore. For more information, see the Apache website, http://hadoop.apache.org.

To perform both read and write operations in native mode, install the required third-party client software. For example, install the Oracle client to connect to the Oracle database.

Verify that the Big Data Management administrator user can run pseudo commands or have user root privileges.

Verify that the temporary folder on the node has at least 2 GB of disk space.

Verify that the destination directory for Informatica binary files is empty.

Verify connection requirements. Verify the connection to the Hadoop cluster nodes, that is, NameNode→DataNodes.

Note: Big Data Management requires a Secure Shell (SSH) connection without a password between the machine where you want to run the Big Data Management installation and all the nodes in the Hadoop cluster. Configure passwordless SSH for the root user. For security reasons, consider removing the passwordless SSH configuration for the root user when Big Data Management installation and configuration are complete.

TUTORIAL: INSTALLING IN A CLUSTER ENVIRONMENT FROM THE PRIMARY NAME NODE USING SCP PROTOCOL

You can install Big Data Management in a cluster environment from the primary name node using SCP.

1. Log in to the primary NameNode.

2. Run the following command to start the Big Data Management installation in console mode:

   bash InformaticaHadoopInstall.sh.

3. Press y to accept the Big Data Management terms of agreement.

4. Press Enter.

5. Press 2 to install Big Data Management in a cluster environment.

6. Press Enter.

7. Type the absolute path for the Big Data Management installation directory.

    Start the path with a slash. The directory names in the path must not contain spaces or the following special characters:

    { } ! @ # $ % ^ & * ( ) : ; | ' ` < > , + [ ] \

    If you type a directory path that does not exist, the installer creates the entire directory path on each of the nodes during the installation.
    Default is /opt.

8. Press Enter.

9. Press 1 to install Big Data Management from the primary name node.

10. Press Enter.

11. Type the absolute path for the Hadoop installation directory. Start the path with a slash.

12. Press Enter.

13. Type y.

14. Press Enter.

The installer retrieves a list of DataNodes from the $HADOOP_HOME/conf/slaves file. On each of the DataNodes, the installer creates the Informatica directory and populates all of the file systems with the contents of the RPM package. The Informatica directory is located here:

/<BigDataManagementInstallationDirectory>/Informatica.

You can view the informatica-hadoop-install. <DateTimeStamp>. log installation log file to get more information about the tasks performed by the installer.

CHAPTER 6

Big Data Repository

OVERVIEW

The world of structured, semi-structured, and un-structured data is comprised of two **Data Management Use Cases.** We know that data is the business asset for any organization that always keeps it secured and accessible to business users whenever required. In the current era, two techniques are very popular to store data for business insights. Hence, we are going to differentiate between them based on some technical terms.

1. **Data Warehouse**, which is the highly structured store of the data that is requiring a significant amount of discovery, planning, data modeling, and development work before the data becomes available for analysis by the business users.

2. **Data Lake**, which is a storage repository that holds a vast amount of raw data in its native format, including structured, semi-structured, and un-structured data. The data structure and requirements are not defined until the data is needed. We can say that the Data Lake is a more organic store of data without regard for the perceived value or structure of the data.

Data Warehouses versus Data Lakes – Depending on the business requirements, a typical organization will require both a data warehouse and a Data Lake as they serve different needs and use cases. The following table provides a side-by-side comparison of their characteristics.

Characteristics	Data Warehouse	Data Lake
Type of data stored	Structured data (most often in columns and rows in a relational database) from transactional systems, operational databases, and line of business applications	Any type of data structure, any format, including structured, semi-structured, and un-structured data from IoT devices, websites, mobile apps, social media, and corporate applications
Best way to ingest data	Batch processes or MapReduce processes	Streaming, micro-batch, or batch processes
Schema	Designed prior to the DW implementation (**schema-on-write**)	Define the structure of the data at the time of analysis, referred to as schema on reading (**schema-on-read**)
Typical load pattern	**ETL** – (Extract, Transform, then Load)	**ELT** – (Extract, Load, and Transform at the time the data is loaded)
Price/Performance	Fastest query results using higher-cost storage	Query results getting faster using low-cost storage
Data quality	Highly curated data that serves as the central version of the truth	Any data that may or may not be curated (i.e., raw data)
Users	Business analysts, Business stakeholders	Data scientists, Data developers, and Business analysts (using curated data)
Analytics pattern	Determine structure, acquire data, then analyze it; iterate back to change structure as needed. Batch reporting, BI dashboards, and visualizations	Acquire data, analyze it, then iterate to determine its final structured form Machine Learning, Predictive analytics, data discovery, and profiling

During the development of a traditional data warehouse, we should invest a considerable amount of time analyzing data sources, understanding business processes, profiling data, and modeling data. In contrast, the default expectation for a Data Lake is to acquire all of the data and retain all of the data in their own formats and at the time of data analysis use data visualization tools like Tableau and data virtualization tools like Denodo.

DATA REPOSITORY LAYER

The Big Data management layer includes core tools to integrate, govern, and secure Big Data.[10] This layer supports pre-built connectors from data visualization tools and data transformations, data quality, data lineage, and data masking such as data vault, which masks data from most users except those who are authorized to access the data realm. Here, the emphasis should be on ensuring data is made fit-for-purpose and protected in an automated, flexible, and scalable repository such as HIVE or HBase.

As the traditional ETL struggled with Big Data, a new distributed data storage and processing system evolved: Apache Hadoop, built from the ground up to be massively scalable (thousands of servers) using standard hardware. In addition, Hadoop is very flexible in terms of data type, format, and structure.

As we have seen in Figure 5.2, Big Data ETL revolves around Hadoop, which apart from being cost effective, provides scalability and flexibility out of the box. Hadoop's architecture is comprised of two major components, HDFS – massive redundant data storage based on HDFS replication factor and MapReduce, scalable batch data processing.

In cases where data volume is high, transformations are slowing down the R-DBMSs that also face bottlenecks on query performance. Transformations are much better suited for a batch processing system like Hadoop which offers the agility to work with any data type, and are very scalable.

As we have seen, there are data management tools like Informatica that provide ETL capabilities for Hadoop using

MapReduce. This allows reusing business transformation logic and defines it through the ETL tool, then enables ETL execution to happen in Hadoop.

HIVE BIG DATA WAREHOUSE

Cloudera HIVE is a data warehouse infrastructure built on top of Hadoop for providing data summarization, query, and analytics. Cloudera HIVE supports analysis of large datasets stored in Hadoop's HDFS and compatible file systems such as the Amazon S3 filesystem. It provides an SQL-like language called HIVEQL (HIVE Query Language) while maintaining full support for MapReduce. HIVEQL or IMPALA can be used to query data stored in various databases and file systems that integrate with Hadoop. Tools like Informatica's Big Data Management use ETL Connector for HIVE that loads data using MapReduce into Hive data warehouse.

In summary, data management tools such as Informatica Big Data Management provide the fast and efficient means to automate Big Data feeds (using MapReduce parallel processing) into data warehouses such as HIVE or HBase. The data repository needs to be one that has data warehouse constructs and supports a wide variety of BI connectors and data query tools for performing data analytics.

Strengths for HIVE:

- Supports STAR schema

- Supports large tables that may also be stored externally on HDFS storage

- Supports data warehouse constructs such as FACT tables, DIMENSION tables, and DIMENSION hierarchies for data roll-ups and drill-downs

- Supports slowly changing dimensions (see Figure 6.1)

- Wide variety of BI connectors from data visualization tools and data query tools for performing data analytics

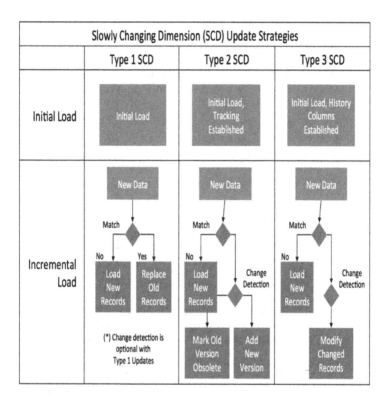

Slowly Changing Dimension (SCD) Update Strategies		
	Type 1 SCD	Type 2 SCD	Type 3 SCD
Initial Load	Initial Load	Initial Load, Tracking Established	Initial Load, History Columns Established
Incremental Load	New Data — Match — No: Load New Records / Yes: Replace Old Records (*) Change detection is optional with Type 1 Updates	New Data — Match — No: Load New Records / Change Detection → Mark Old Version Obsolete / Add New Version	New Data — Match — No: Load New Records / Change Detection → Modify Changed Records

FIGURE 6.1   Slowly changing dimension in HIVE. (From hive.apache.org.)

SLOWLY CHANGING DIMENSION IN HIVE

The HIVE data repository supports multi-dimensional STAR schema for OLAP. An essential element in Ralph Kimball's multi-dimensional data model were different approaches to capture the history of slowly changing dimensions. Figure 6.1 shows how these approaches are implemented in HIVE.[10]

TUTORIAL: HIVE DATA STRUCTURES

The **HIVE** metastore is a service that stores the **metadata** for **HIVE** tables and partitions in a relational database. It provides clients (including **HIVE**) access to this information using the metastore service API.

HIVE stores data inside /hive/warehouse default folder on HDFS if no other directory is specified using a location tag while creating the HIVE table. It is stored in various formats. HIVE data inside the HIVE table can be accessed through HIVEQL as well as through PIG.

There are two types of tables in HIVE: one is a **managed** table and the second one is an **external** table.

The primary difference is:

- When we drop a managed table, HIVE deletes both data and metadata.

- When we drop an external table, HIVE only deletes metadata; this is a way to protect data in external tables against accidental drop commands.

  - Syntax for managed table creation:

    create table managedemp(col1 datatype,col2 datatype, ...) row format delimited fields terminated by 'delimiter character' location '/data/employee';

  - Syntax for external table creation:

    create external table extemp(col1 datatype,col2 datatype, ...) row format delimited fields terminated by 'delimiter character' location '/data/employee';

    Please note the LOCATION tag which is used to specify the fully qualified directory on the HDFS server where the table data will be stored.

  - Check for table creation:

    describe formatted managedemp;

    System response:

    Location: hdfs://10.1.22.14:1088/data/employee,

    where 10.1.22.14 is the I.P. address of NameNode or MasterNode of the Hadoop Cluster and 1088 is the port number of the HIVE database listener.

- Syntax for dropping an external table:

  drop table extemp;

- Check for data file of the external table after the drop:

  hadoop fs -ls hdfs:// 10.1.22.14:1088/data/employee

  System response:

  It will list the data filename because the drop on external table only deletes metadata.

- How to specify HIVE Database Name for "contacts" table

/hive/warehouse/<database name>.db/contacts
where "database name" should be replaced by the actual HIVE database name.

Note: In this example the contacts table was created in the default directory, **/hive/warehouse** because the LOCATION tag was not used in the creation of the "contacts" table.

HIVE METADATA: DEFINITIONS

Metadata, in general, refers to data about the data. From the HIVE standpoint as part of the Hadoop Eco system, this can mean one of many things. To list a few, metadata can refer to:

1. *Metadata about logical datasets.* This includes information like the location of a dataset (e.g., directory in HDFS or the HIVE table name), schema associated with the data- set for partitioning, and sorting properties of the dataset. Such metadata is usually stored in a separate metadata repository.

2. *Metadata about files under HDFS directories.* This includes information like permissions and ownership of such files,

location of various blocks of that file on DataNodes, etc. <u>Such information is usually stored and managed by the Hadoop NameNode.</u>

3. *Metadata about tables in HIVE.* This includes information like table names, associated namespace, associated attributes (e.g., MAX_FILESIZE, READONLY, etc.), names of column families, etc. Such information is stored and managed by the HIVE data warehouse itself.

4. *Metadata about data ingestion and transformations.* This includes information like which user generated a given dataset, where did the dataset come from, how long did it take to generate it, how many records or alternatively, what was the size of the data loaded.

5. *Metadata about dataset statistics.* This includes information like number of rows in a dataset, number of unique values in each column, histogram of the distribution of data, and maximum and minimum values. Such metadata is useful for various tools that can leverage it for optimizing their execution plans but also for data analysts who can do quick analysis based on it.

What is the importance of metadata?

1. It allows one to interact with data through the higher level logical abstraction of a table rather than as a mere collection of files on HDFS or a table in HIVE. This means that the users don't need to be concerned about where or how the data is stored.

2. It allows one to supply information about their data (e.g., partitioning or sorting properties) that can then be leveraged by various tools to enforce them while populating data and leverage them when querying data.

3. It allows data management tools to "hook" into this metadata and allows one to perform data discovery (discover what data is available and how you can use it) and lineage (trace back where a given dataset came from or originated) analysis.

4. The HIVE metastore tracks DDL activities, which means a simple CREATE TABLE command creates the metadata, while an ALTER TABLE command alters the metadata and user queries on the tables use the information in HIVE metastore.

Where is metadata stored?

The first project in the Hadoop Eco system that started storing, managing, and leveraging metadata was Cloudera HIVE. HIVE stores this metadata in a relational database called the HIVE metastore. Please note that HIVE also includes a service called the HIVE metastore service that interfaces with the HIVE metastore database.

Therefore:

HIVE metastore = HIVE metastore database
+ HIVE metastore service

The HIVE metastore can be accessed by the HCatalog using a REST API via the WebHCat server. One can think of the HCatalog as an access layer around HIVE metastore. For security concerns, WebHCat server allows the cluster administrators to lock down access to the Hive metastore.

TUTORIAL: HIVE INSTALLATION, ENVIRONMENT AND ARCHITECTURE[11]

```
# Set HIVE_HOME
hadoop fs -export HIVE_HOME="/usr/lib/hive"
```

#On the HDFS server go to HIVE_HOME
```
hadoop fs -cd /usr/lib/hive
```

#Check for the "tar" file
```
hadoop fs -ls apache-hive-1.2.0-bin.tar.gz
```

#Extract the "tar" file
```
hadoop fs -gunzip apache-hive-1.2.0-bin.tar.gz
hadoop fs -tar -xvf  apache-hive-1.2.0-bin.tar
```

The code tree for HIVE is installed under the HIVE_HOME,"/usr/lib/hive"

#Include HIVE code tree in the HDFS Server PATH
```
hadoop fs -PATH=$PATH:$HIVE_HOME/bin
hadoop fs -export PATH
```

Mention the HADOOP_HOME Path in hive-config.sh file as shown in below (HADOOP_HOME Path)
```
hadoop fs -export HADOOP_HOME=$HIVE_HOME/YARN/
hadoop-2.2.0
hadoop fs -PATH=$PATH:$HADOOP_HOME
hadoop fs -export PATH
```

#Example to create HIVE directory
```
hadoop fs -mkdir $HIVE_HOME/warehouse
```

#Assign proper permissions on HIVE directory created above
```
hadoop fs -chmod g+w $HIVE_HOME/warehouse
```

#Execute HIVE executable to get into HIVE shell
```
hadoop fs -$HIVE_HOME/bin/hive
```

Use MYSQL as metastorage at the back end to connect multiple users with HIVE at a time.

#Install "mysql" database

Since all environment variables are set,
```
hadoop fs -cd $HIVE_HOME
sudo apt-get install mysql-server
```

#It will prompt for sudo password for the HDFS server, i.e., HIVE server
```
< type in the sudo password for the HIVE server >
```

#Install "mysql" Java connector
```
sudo apt-get install libmysql-java
<creates /usr/share/java/mysql-connector-java.jar
file>
jar xvf /usr/share/java/mysql-connector-java.jar
<extracts contents and places them in proper
directories>
```

#Create Java softlink connector in HIVE directory.
#This is for soft link between Java and MySql.
```
ls -s /usr/share/java/mysql-connector-java.jar
$HIVE_HOME/lib/mysql-connector-java.jar
```

#Configure "mysql" in HIVE
#Log into "mysql" shell
```
mysql -u root -p
```

<Here –u represents root or an username with root privilege, p denotes root password. Once you enter "mysql", you will see the prompt "mysql>" just like "SQL>" prompt in Oracle>.

#Create USER in "mysql"
```
mysql> create user 'hiveguru'@'%' identified by
'password';
```

#Grant privileges in "mysql"
```
mysql> grant all on *.* to hiveguru @localhost
identified by 'password';
```

#Use HIVE metastore
```
mysql> use metastore <note this command is not
terminated by ';'>
mysql> show tables;
```

#Configuring hive-site.xml
```
hadoop fs -mkdir $HIVE_HOME/conf
hadoop fs -export HIVE_CONF_DIR=$HIVE_HOME/conf
```

```
hadoop fs -cd $HIVE_HOME/conf
hadoop fs -gedit hive-site.xml
```

The code for the four properties are given in the XML configuration file below. <u>The property definitions are as follows</u>:

1. The first property is for the connection URL purpose. Here we are defining a connection URL in this property. It acts as a JDBC connection and it is representing the metastore location as well.

2. The second property is for the connection driver name. Here, mysql.jdbc.Driver is the respected value we have to mention in the value tag.

3. The third property is used for defining the connection user name. In this, we defined "hiveguru" as user name.

4. The fourth property is used for mentioning the connection password. In this, we defined password as user password.

This code must be placed in hive-site.xml.

```
<configuration>
        <property>
                <name>javax.jdo.option.
ConnectionURL</name>
                <value>jdbc:mysql://localhost/metas
tore?createDatabaseIfNotExist=true</value>
                <description>metadata is stored in
a MySQL server</description>
        </property>
        <property>
                <name>javax.jdo.option.
ConnectionDriverName</name>
                <value>com.mysql.jdbc.Driver
</value>
                <description>MySQL JDBC driver
class</description>
        </property>
        <property>
```

```
                <name>javax.jdo.option.
ConnectionUserName</name>
                <value>hiveuser</value>
                <description>user name for
connecting to mysql server</description>
        </property>
        <property>
                <name>javax.jdo.option.
ConnectionPassword</name>
                <value>hivepassword</value>
                <description>password for
connecting to mysql server</description>
        </property>
</configuration>
```

#Create table "students" in HIVE
```
hive> create table students(id int, name string);
```

The column names mentioned with its data type as an integer, and another one is with the string type data.

In the next step, we are going to check whether it is stored in MySQL or not.

\# Entering into MySQL shell mode. We now know how to do that: mysql –u root –p.

\# Following that use the steps given below.

```
mysql> use metastore
mysql> show tables;
mysql> select * from TBLS;
```

To recollect,

• First we have to use the database as "use metastore."

• Once it chooses the metastore we can check the tables present in this by using "show" tables command as shown above.

• Whatever the tables that are created in HIVE, the metadata corresponds to the tables that are stored under TBLS in MySQL database (Figure 6.2).

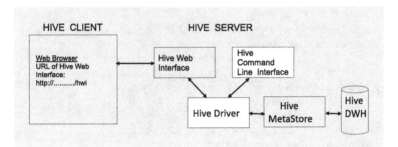

FIGURE 6.2   High-level HIVE architecture.

We have seen in the tutorial on data migration where Apache SQOOP uses HIVE Command Line Interface on the Hadoop server to import the Oracle-R-DBMS table into the HIVE Data Warehouse. The HIVE driver can also be invoked by the HIVE Client on a web browser using the HIVE Web Interface. As a security measure the WebHCat server allows the Hadoop cluster administrators to control access to the HIVE Metastore. We cannot overemphasize that no queries can be made to the HIVE Data Warehouse without being validated by the HIVE Metastore.

INTEGRATED USE OF DATA INTEGRATION, DATA MANAGEMENT, AND DATA VISUALIZATION TOOLS

The aforementioned architecture schematic shows how Informatica BDM joins hands with HIVE Big Data Warehouse, which uses HDFS and MapReduce processing to bring over the source system data (Figure 6.3). The source system data can be in the form of:

- Structured data such as R-DBMS tables.

- Semi-structured data such as Java Script Object Notation (JSON) datasets in NoSQL databases like Mongo.

- Un-structured web log files or click-stream data.

This data is stored as a managed table or external table in the HIVE Big Data Warehouse as a persistent data store.

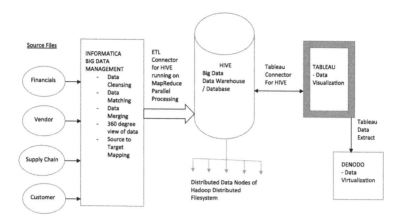

FIGURE 6.3   Big Data architecture – high performance/high quality/ fault tolerant.

As shown in the schematic, for BI data analytics the Tableau connector for HIVE can be used to slice and dice the data stored in the HIVE repository. Denodo can be used to bring the data in the Data Lake to the same level of abstraction for meaningful data analytics.

CHAPTER 7

Big Data Visualization

OVERVIEW

The scale, velocity, and scope of data today demands visualization/ reporting tools that deploy quickly. The requirements for these tools are:

1. They should connect using BI connectors to a wide variety of data sources given below:
   a. Hadoop databases that mine massive amounts of data.
   b. NoSQL databases that are enabling social media giants like Facebook to mine massive, multi-petabyte data streams.
2. They should guide the users to use the best techniques such as R programming and data wrangling for rendering data into information that provides business value. For more information on R programming language, visit http:// www.r-project.org.
3. They must be suitable for non-technical users.
4. They should avoid characteristics of traditional BI tools that had surprisingly low adoption rates of around 8%.[12]

At the heart of Tableau is a proprietary technology that makes interactive data visualization an integral part of understanding data. It is naturally an analysis tool that forces us to analyze data in rows and columns, and then organize that data into visual presentations. The strong point is that it has out-of-the-box BI connectors/APIs to NoSQL and Hadoop Big Data databases.

The ideal analytics and reporting tool should possess the following characteristics:

1. Simplicity: Be easy for non-technical users to master.

2. Connectivity: Seamlessly connect to a large variety of data sources.

3. Visual competence: Provide built-in graphics of high business value.

4. Sharing: Facilitate sharing of insights.

5. Scale: Handle large datasets.

TUTORIAL: TEXT ANALYTICS – R PROGRAMMING

This data science tutorial introduces the viewer to the exciting world of text analytics with R programming. As exemplified by the popularity of blogging and social media, textual data is far from dead – it is increasing exponentially![13]

There is a world of R programming that is used in text analytics which can't be addressed here as it is beyond the scope of this tutorial. For a comprehensive review of R programming, please visit http://www.r-project.org.

To capture the essential commands in R programming, for starters, we will cover just the basic topics dealing with data manipulation of variables, strings, numbers, tables, factors, and files.

The numbers within the c command are separated by commas. As an example, we can create a new variable, called "bubba", which will contain the numbers 3, 5, 7, and 9.

Create and load data into variable:

```
> bubba <- c(3,5,7,9)
```

If you wish to work with one of the numbers you can get access to it using the variable and then square brackets indicating which number:

```
> bubba[2]
[1] 5
> bubba[1]
[1] 3
```

Notice that the first entry is referred to as the number 1 entry, and the zero entry can be used to indicate how the computer will treat the data. You can store strings using both single and double quotes, and you can store real numbers.

It is rare to have just a few data points that you do not mind typing in at the prompt. It is much more common to have a lot of data points with complicated relationships. Here we will examine how to read a dataset from a file using the read.csv function but first discuss the format of a data file.

The data file is called simple.csv, and has three columns of data and six rows. The three columns are labeled "trial," "mass," and "velocity." We can pretend that each row comes from an observation during one of two trials labeled "A" and "B."

Create a matrix, heisenberg, and load data from a file, simple.csv into it.

The file layout for simple.csv is given below:

Trial	Mass	Velocity
A	10	12
A	11	14
B	5	8
B	6	10
A	10.5	13
B	7	11

```
> heisenberg <- read.csv(file="simple.
csv",head=TRUE,sep=",")
> heisenberg
```

```
trial mass velocity
1    A 10.0        12
2    A 11.0        14
3    B  5.0         8
4    B  6.0        10
5    A 10.5        13
6    B  7.0        11
```

sep: separator is ","

Create a summary of the matrix, `heisenberg`

```
> summary(heisenberg)
trial       mass            velocity
A:3   Min.   : 5.00   Min.   : 8.00
B:3   1st Bu.: 6.25   1st Qu.:10.25
      Median : 8.50   Median :11.50
      Mean   : 8.25   Mean   :11.33
      3rd Qu.:10.38   3rd Qu.:12.75
      Max.   :11.00   Max.   :14.00
```

dir() command to list the files

```
> dir()
[1] "fixedWidth.dat" "simple.csv"  "trees91.csv"
"trees91.wk1"
[5] "w1.dat"
```

getwd() command to determine the current working directory

```
> getwd()
[1] "/home/black/write/class/stat/stat383-13F/dat"
```

The variable "heisenberg" contains the three columns of data. Each column is assigned a name based on the header (the first line in the file). You can now access each individual column using a "$" to separate the two names:

matrix$column-name

Where matrix is recently loaded "heisenberg," and column names are "trial mass", and "velocity."

```
> heisenberg$trial
[1] A A B B A B
Levels: A B
> heisenberg$mass
[1] 10.0 11.0  5.0  6.0 10.5  7.0
> heisenberg$velocity
[1] 12 14  8 10 13 11
```

How to find column names in the recently loaded "heisenberg." If you are not sure what columns are contained in the variable, you can use the names command:

```
> names(heisenberg)
[1] "trial"    "mass"     "velocity"
```

The original data is given in an Excel spreadsheet, and the .CSV file, trees91.csv, was created by deleting the top set of rows and saving it as a "csv" file. This is an option to save within Excel (You should save the file on your computer.). It is a good idea to open this file in a spreadsheet and look at it. This will help you make sense of how R programming stores the data.

A section of the sample file, trees91.csv is presented below to demonstrate the following commands in R programing language: read.csv, attributes, names, and so on.

C	N	CHBR	REP	LFBM	STBM	RTBM	LFNCC	STNCC	RTNCC	LFBCC
1	1	CL6	1	0.43	0.13	0.29	1.84	0.4	0.96	39
1	1	CL7	1	0.4	0.15	0.25	1.82	0.37	0.95	36
1	2	A1	9	0.45	0.2	0.21	1.54	0.96	0.69	34
1	2	A1	14	0.82	0.26	0.29	1.75	0.97	0.83	34
1	2	A1	20	0.52	0.19	0.25	2.01	1.29	0.8	34
1	2	A7		1.32	0.46	0.48	1.45	0.92	0.72	28
1	3	A3		0.9	0.42	0.47	1.8	1.19	0.84	33
1	3	D5		1.18	0.53	0.78	1.53	0.84	0.77	40
2	1	A4	9	0.48	0.2	0.28	1.58	0.89	0.98	41
2	1	A4	14	0.21	0.07	0.22	1.26	0.66	0.77	41
2	1	A4	20	0.27	0.13	0.24	1.88	1.28	1.19	41

(Continued)

C	N	CHBR	REP	LFBM	STBM	RTBM	LFNCC	STNCC	RTNCC	LFBCC
2	1	B3	9	0.31	0.14	0.21	2.76	0.64	0.84	41
2	1	B3	14	0.65	0.18	0.3	1.49	0.64	0.78	41
2	1	B3	20	0.18	0.1	0.12	1.38	0.64	0.91	41
2	1	B6	9	0.52	0.18	0.38	1.3	0.79	0.78	41
2	1	B6	14	0.3	0.14	0.24	1.69	0.79	0.78	41
2	1	B6	20	0.58	0.19	0.31	2.12	0.79	0.78	41
2	2	A5		0.48	0.2	0.29	1.82	0.95	0.8	44
2	2	B4	9	0.58	0.2	0.78	1.39	0.98	0.6	47
2	2	B4	14	0.58	0.2	0.78	1.32	0.98	0.6	47
2	2	B4	20	0.41	0.1	0.52	2.02	0.98	0.6	47
2	2	B7	9	0.48	0.16	0.29	1.68	0.96	0.81	36
2	2	B7	14	1.76	0.53	0.35	1.91	0.96	0.81	36
2	2	B7	20	1.21	0.27	0.28	2.07	0.96	0.81	36
2	3	A2	1	1.18	0.48	0.55	1.73	0.75	0.71	40
2	3	A6	9	0.83	0.3	0.45	1.23	0.86	0.74	37
2	3	A6	14	1.22	0.55	0.5	1.61	0.94	0.47	37
2	3	A6	20	0.77	0.27	0.34	1.35	0.89	0.83	37
2	3	B5	9	1.02	0.47	1.51	1.53	0.92	0.58	48
2	3	B5	14	0.13	0.03	0.15	1.8	0.92	0.58	48
2	3	B5	20	0.68	0.27	0.95	2.09	0.92	0.58	48
3	1	B1	20	0.61	0.22	0.28	1.68	1.05	0.62	34
3	1	B2	9	0.7	0.24	0.38	1.14	0.63	0.51	34
3	1	B2	14	0.82	0.33	0.67	1.56	0.63	0.51	34
3	1	B2	20	0.76	0.37	0.47	1.8	0.63	0.51	34
3	1	D2	20	0.77	0.32	0.46	1.62	0.71	0.76	35
3	3	C1		1.69	0.72	0.96	1.67	0.87	0.79	25
3	3	C2	9	1.48	0.6	0.54	1.58	0.78	0.62	30
3	3	C2	14	0.74	0.2	0.5	1.43	0.78	0.75	30

The data can be read into a variable called "tree" in using the read.csv command:

```
> tree <-read.csv(file="trees91.csv",header=
TRUE,sep=",");
```

This will create a new variable called "tree." If you type in "tree" at the prompt and hit enter, all of the numbers stored in the variable will be printed out. Try this, and you should see that it is difficult to make any sense out of the numbers.

There are many different ways to keep track of data in R. When you use the read.csv command, R uses a specific kind of variable called a "data frame." All of the data are stored within the data frame as separate columns. If you are not sure what kind of variable you have then you can use the attributes command. This will list all of the things that R uses to describe the variable:

```
> attributes(tree)
$names
 [1] "C"       "N"       "CHBR"    "REP"     "LFBM"
"STBM"   "RTBM"   "LFNCC"
 [9] "STNCC"  "RTNCC"  "LFBCC"   "STBCC"   "RTBCC"
"LFCACC" "STCACC" "RTCACC"
[17] "LFKCC"  "STKCC"  "RTKCC"   "LFMGCC"  "STMGCC"
"RTMGCC" "LFPCC"  "STPCC"
[25] "RTPCC"  "LFSCC"  "STSCC"   "RTSCC"
```

These are the column headings of the spreadsheet, trees91.csv. There are 54 rows in the spreadsheet

```
$class
[1] "data.frame"

$row.names
 [1] "1"   "2"   "3"   "4"   "5"   "6"   "7"   "8"   "9"
"10" "11" "12" "13" "14" "15"
[16] "16" "17" "18" "19" "20" "21" "22" "23" "24"
"25" "26" "27" "28" "29" "30"
[31] "31" "32" "33" "34" "35" "36" "37" "38" "39"
"40" "41" "42" "43" "44" "45"
[46] "46" "47" "48" "49" "50" "51" "52" "53" "54"
```

If you want to work with the data in one of the columns, you give the name of the data frame, a "$" sign, and the label assigned to the column. For example, the first column in tree can be called using "tree$C".

To list first column, C:

```
> tree$C
[1] 1 1 1 1 1 1 1 1 2 2 2 2 2 2 2 2 2 2 2 2 2 2 2 2
2 2 2 2 2 2 2 3 3 3 3 3 3 3 3 3
```

To list second column, N:

```
> tree$N
[1] 1 1 2 2 2 2 3 3 1 1 1 1 1 1 1 1 1 1 2 2 2 2 2 2
3 3 3 3 3 3 3 1 1 1 1 1 3 3 3
```

Brief Note on Fixed Width Files

There are many ways to read data using R. We only give two examples: direct assignment and reading .csv files. However, another way deserves a brief mention. It is common to come across data that is organized in flat files and delimited at preset locations on each line. This is often called a "fixed width file."

The command to deal with these kind of files is read.fwf (read fixed width file). Examples of how to use this command are not explored here, but a brief example is given. If you would like more information on how to use this command enter the following command:

```
> help(read.fwf)
```

The command to deal with these kinds of files is read.fwf. Examples of how to use this command are not explored here, but a brief example is given. If you would like more information on how to use this command enter the following command:

```
> help(read.fwf)   [ fixed width file (fwf) ]
```

The read.fwf command requires at least two options. The first is the name of the file and the second is a list of numbers that gives the length of each column in the data file. A negative number in the list indicates that the column should be skipped. Here we give the command to read the data file fixedwidth.dat. In this data file there are three columns. The first column is 17 characters wide, the second column is 15 characters wide, and the last column is 7 characters wide. In the example below we use the optional col. names option to specify the names of the columns:

Populate 'a':

```
> a = read.fwf('fixedWidth.dat',
widths=c(17,15,7),col.names=c('temp', 'offices'))
```

List contents of 'a':

```
> a
  temp offices
1 17.0      35
2 18.0     117
3 17.5      19
4 17.5      28
```

We look at some of the ways that R can store and organize data. This is a basic introduction to a small subset of the different data types recognized by R and is not comprehensive in any sense. The main goal is to demonstrate the different kinds of information R can handle. It is assumed that you know how to enter data or read data files, which is covered in the first chapter.

VARIABLE TYPES

Numbers

The way to work with real numbers has already been covered in the first chapter and is briefly discussed here. The most basic way to store a number is to make an assignment of a single number:

```
> a <- 3
>
```

The "<-" tells R to take the number to the right of the symbol and store it in a variable whose name is given on the left. You can also use the "=" symbol. When you make an assignment, R does not print out any information. If you want to see what value a variable has, just type the name of the variable on a line and press the enter key:

```
> a
[1] 3
```

This allows you to do all sorts of basic operations and save the numbers:

```
> b <- sqrt(a*a+3)
> b
[1] 3.464102
```

If you want to get a list of the variables that you have defined in a particular session, you can list them all using the l's command:

```
> ls()
[1] "a" "b"
```

You are not limited to just saving a single number. You can create a list (also called a "vector") using the c command:

```
> a <- c(1,2,3,4,5)
> a
[1] 1 2 3 4 5
> a+1
[1] 2 3 4 5 6
> mean(a)
[1] 3
> var(a)
[1] 2.5
```

You can get access to particular entries in the vector in the following manner:

```
> a <- c(1,2,3,4,5)
> a[1]
```

```
[1] 1
> a[2]
[1] 2
> a[0]
numeric(0)
> a[5]
[1] 5
> a[6]
[1] NA
```

Note that the zero entry is used to indicate how the data is stored. The first entry in the vector is the first number, and if you try to get a number past the last number you get "NA."

Examples of the sort of operations you can do on vectors is given in the next chapter.

To initialize a list of numbers, the *numeric* command can be used. For example, to create a list of 10 numbers, initialized to zero, use the following command:

```
> a <- numeric(10)
> a
[1] 0 0 0 0 0 0 0 0 0 0
```

If you wish to determine the data type used for a variable, use the *type* command:

```
> typeof(a)
[1] "double"
```

Strings

You are not limited to just storing numbers. You can also store strings. A string is specified by using quotes. Both single and double quotes will work:

```
> a <- "hello"
> a
[1] "hello"
> b <- c("hello","there")
```

```
> b
[1] "hello" "there"
> b[1]
[1] "hello"
```

The name of the type given to strings is character:

```
> typeof(a)
[1] "character"
> a = character(20)
> a
[1] "" "" "" "" "" "" "" "" "" "" "" "" "" "" ""
"" "" "" "" ""
```

Factors

Another important way R can store data is as a factor. Often times an experiment includes trials for different levels of some explanatory variable. For example, when looking at the impact of carbon dioxide on the growth rate of a tree, you might try to observe how different trees grow when exposed to different preset concentrations of carbon dioxide. The different levels are also called factors.

Assuming you know how to read in a file, we will look at the data file given in the first chapter. Several of the variables in the file are factors:

```
> summary(tree$CHBR)
A1   A2   A3   A4   A5   A6   A7   B1   B2   B3   B4   B5
B6   B7   C1   C2   C3   C4   C5   C6
3    1    1    3    1    3    1    1    3    3    3    3
3    3    1    3    1    3    1    1
C7  CL6  CL7   D1   D2   D3   D4   D5   D6   D7
1    1    1    1    1    3    1    1    1    1
```

Because the set of options given in the data file corresponding to the "CHBR" column are not all numbers, R automatically assumes that it is a **factor**.

SUCCESS FACTORS FOR TABLEAU

Tableau is one of the most popular and widely used business intelligence tools positioned by Gartner's magic quadrant last year. Consisting of highly advanced data visualization features, users can create, display and share interactive reports in almost no time. Serving over 23,000 customers across the globe, this tool is pretty easy to use and requires a lesser amount of technical expertise. The abilities of blending datasets, collaborating in real time, and platform independence makes it a highly desirable business intelligence technology. Tableau works on an n-tier client-server architecture that supports fast and dynamic deployments.[14]

Below are the several servers that manage the internal processes of Tableau (see Figure 7.1).

- **Gateway/Load Balancer** – A point of entry to the Tableau server and balances the process load.

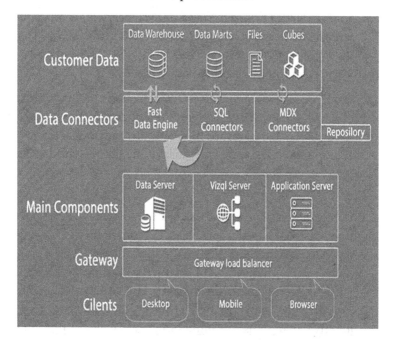

FIGURE 7.1   Tableau architecture. (From www.progress.com.)

- **Application Server** – Authenticates the permission for any user for the Tableau Server web and mobile interfaces.

- **Repository** – A PostgreSQL database storing server data.

- **VIZQL Server** – Processes the request, sends it to data source, and provides the outputs.

- **Data Engine** – Stores the data and extracts the answers for the queries.

- **Backgrounder** – Executes the server tasks.

- **DataServer** – Maintains the connection between Tableau server and data sources.

TABLEAU: STEP FORWARD IN DATA ANALYTICS

Tableau is the data visualization tool that uncovers the three kinds of data that exist in every business entity.[15]

1. Known Data (Type 1): These daily, weekly, and monthly reports are used for monitoring activity. These reports are used to FRAME questions and NOT ANSWER questions. They only provide visibility of operations.

2. Data you knew but you need to know in a certain context (Type 2): Once patterns and outliers emerge in Type 1 data, the question that is framed is: Why is this happening? For any action to be taken, first the cause of the outliers need to be understood. Traditional reporting tools provide a framework to build the above understanding.

3. Data you don't know that you need to know (Type 3): Real-time visual analytics provides the possibility of seeing patterns and outliers that are not visible in Type 1 and Type 2 data. The process of interacting with granular data yields different questions that can lead to new actionable insights. The software that enables quick and real-time iterative analysis is becoming a necessary element of data visualization.

Advantages of Tableau[16]

- **Everyone can use** – Tableau allows a common user to generate the interactive business intelligence reports even with lesser technical expertise. Tableau is perfectly suitable for top management employees who need a smart business intelligence tool that is easy to operate.

- **Fast** – Tableau is able to create interactive visualizations and reports in a few minutes that makes it a very fast tool.

TUTORIAL: TABLEAU – REAL-TIME DASHBOARD

- **Maps** – Tableau is very efficient in creating multi-dimensional maps with the help of its built-in geo-coding feature.

- **Interactive data visualization** – Tableau prepares interactive reports and provides recommendations according to the user requirements. Tableau is rich in data visualization capabilities, and due to this it automatically segments data into measures and segments.

- **Time and effort saving** – Using Tableau, one can easily connect to the database which reduces time and effort of the user that can be used in analytics.

- **Cost effective** – Not only time and effort saving, this technology saves money as well because this tool let the companies avoid investing money in acquiring additional IT resources.

- **Sharing of information** – Tableau creates as well as allows sharing the reports online/offline, making the entire process faster.

- **Maintains security** – Tableau exercises control over the access of information with the help of various security measures (Figure 7.2).

Montclare names Tableau as one of the Top 20 Software as a Service (SaaS) companies. Tableau has invested heavily in Tableau

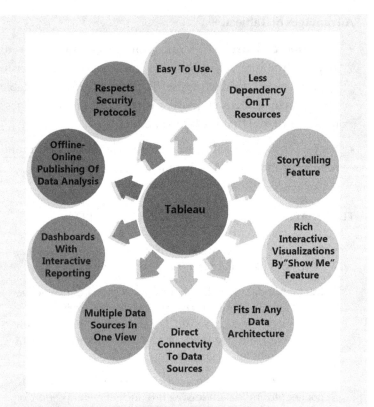

FIGURE 7.2   Features of Tableau. (From community.tableau.com.)

Online, which integrates easily with platforms like Amazon Web Services, Google Cloud, and Microsoft Azure. Tableau users can also connect to cloud data sources like Amazon Redshift and all kinds of web data. Tableau works with both SOAP and REST web services.[15]

Tableau Online works with all our data, including on-premise data and data in the cloud. Tableau Online can access data from databases, data warehouses, Hadoop clusters, Big Data Warehouse such as HIVE, Excel files, and cloud applications.

Software as a Service business intelligence (SaaS BI) is a delivery model for business intelligence in which applications are typically deployed outside of a company's firewall at a hosted location and accessed by an end user with a secure Internet connection (Figure 7.3).

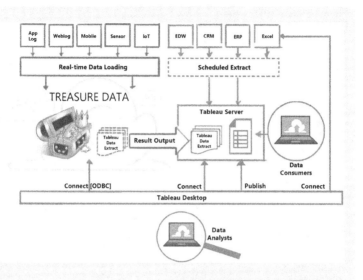

FIGURE 7.3 Tableau SaaS operations. (From tableau.com/solutions.)

The emergence of 3-D dashboards requires access to real-time data. This can be implemented in a couple of ways.[17]

- User initiated data refresh in Tableau Online

- Periodic auto update of data in Tableau Server (uses Java script API)

User Initiated Data Refresh in Tableau Online
Open Professional Tableau Desktop and do the following:

- On Tableau desktop, select **Data** > **Refresh Data Source**

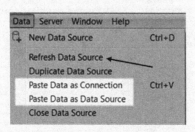

Periodic Auto Update of Data in Tableau Server (Uses Java Script API)

The other approach is to refresh the data in Tableau server. This uses a Java script API (see below).[18]

Set auto refresh of Server data every 3 seconds (3,000 milliseconds)

```
<!DOCTYPE html>
<html lang="en">
<head>
<title>Tableau JavaScript API</title>
<script type="text/javascript"> src="https://\
online.tableausoftware.com/javascripts/api/\
tableau_v8.js">
</script>
</head>
<body>
<div id="tableauViz"></div>

<script type='text/javascript'>
var placeholderDiv = document.
getElementById("tableauViz");
var url = "https://online.tableausoftware.com/t/
shawnwallworktableauonline/views/AutoRefreshTest/\
Dashboard1";
var options = {
hideTabs: true,
width: "100%",
height: "1000px"
};
var viz = new tableauSoftware.Viz(placeholderDiv,
url, options);

setInterval(function () {viz.refreshDataAsync()},
3000);

</script>
</body>
```

TABLEAU CONNECTORS FOR DATA SOURCES

If we want to exploit the potential of the Tableau Visualization tool, it is important to have a clear understanding about its desktop Toolbar menu items.

File Menu: The export packaged workbook option allows one to create a packaged workbook (twbx). Saving the workbook eliminates a couple of clicks. A frequently used feature is the "print to PDF" option. This allows you to export worksheet or dashboard into PDF form.

Data Menu: If you find some tabular data on a website that you want to analyze with Tableau, highlight and copy the data and use the "Paste" option to input into Tableau, which will add it as a data source in the data window.

Worksheet Menu: The export option allows you to export the worksheet as an image to an Excel text table.

TABLEAU DATA ENGINE TUNING

Tableau's Data Engine is an in-memory analytics database that leverages the complete memory hierarchy from disk to L1 cache. It can be a powerful tool for accelerating data analysis. Though it is not built for the same scale as Hadoop, the Tableau Data Engine can deliver low latency results against extracts of data with a cardinality of hundreds of millions of rows and a wide number of columns. Although leveraging extracts in Tableau's Data Engine will usually boost performance out-of-the-box, there are a number of opportunities to accelerate the queries by condensing the size of the data.[19]

Define filters – Create a filter so that you are only focused on the data of interest.

Hide unused fields – Hide fields that are not required for analysis so that the extract is compact and concise.

Aggregate visible dimensions – Pre-aggregate data to a more coarse-grained view when the fine-grained data is not needed to yield the same insights with faster queries.

Roll-up dates – Roll-up dates to coarser-grained timelines when possible.

Sampling – For databases that support it, data sampling can greatly compact the data while still representing the broad trends in the data.

Top N – If you are just looking for the highest values in a dataset, this is an efficient means to reduce the dataset size.

The availability of Tableau Connectors to a wide range of data sources is one of the primary reasons for the popularity of Tableau. All connections start with the professional Tableau Desktop. To connect to Tableau Online, select Tableau Online under Quick Connect. To connect to a Tableau Server, enter the name of the server and then select Connect.

Before one can build a view and analyze data, one must first connect Tableau Desktop to the data source. Tableau supports connecting to a wide variety of data stored in a variety of places. For example, the data might be stored on your computer in a spreadsheet or a text file, or in a Big Data, relational, or cube (multi-dimensional) database on a server in a business enterprise or to a cloud database source, such as Google Analytics, Amazon Redshift, or Salesforce.

Cloudera HIVE is just another data source for Tableau. There are two strategies for importing HIVE data into Tableau:

i. A live connection, which pulls the entire set of data into Tableau and updates on an ongoing basis.

ii. Extracts, in which one selects a subset of Data Lake and pulls it into Tableau.

TUTORIAL: STEPS TO CREATE TABLEAU CONNECTORS

For supported files and databases, Tableau provides built-in connectors that are built and optimized for those types of data. If the file in question or database type is listed under **Connect**, use this named connector to connect to the data. If the file or database type is not listed, one might have the option of creating their own connection using **Other Data Base Connectivity (ODBC)** or **Web Data Connector**. Tableau provides limited support for connections that are user-created using either of these options.

Different information for each data connection needs to be provided. For example, for most data connections, a server name and sign-in information is needed. With some data connections, one can run initial SQL statements, and SSL-enabled servers require that the **"Require SSL" check box is selected** at the time of making the connection. The following sections discuss the specific information we need to provide for each type of data we want to connect to.

Tip – A data source can be quickly created in Tableau by copying and pasting data using the clipboard.[20]

1. Select the data you want and copy it to the clipboard.

2. Open Tableau Desktop and do one of the following:

   - On the data source page, select **Data** > **Paste Data as Connection** or **Paste Data as Data Source**.

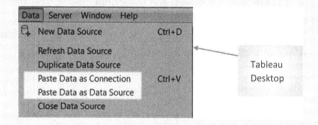

   - On the sheet, select **Data** > **Paste** to paste the data as a data source.

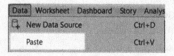

   - Select **File** > **Save** to save the data source.

When one saves the workbook, the data source either becomes a part of the existing data source or is added to the repository, depending on which of the methods is chosen. If you paste the data as a data source, the data source is saved with the workbook when you save the workbook as a packaged workbook (.twbx).

When one signs into the Tableau site and selects New Workbook, the data connectors that are available are shown when you're in the **Connect to Data** window. One can upload files using the **Files** tab, connect to server or cloud data sources with **Connectors**, or use published data sources **on this site**.

If signed into Tableau Online, **Dashboard Starters** are also available. The data connectors supported by the Tableau site are determined by the site's server and the license level. Once connected to data, the connection can be saved to have them show up in the **Data Sources** section of the Tableau site.

REQUEST A NEW CONNECTOR

Although highly unlikely, if Tableau doesn't have a built-in connector for a data source, consider requesting one on the Tableau Community, https://community.tableau.com/. Use Ideas on Community to search for the connector to see if it's been requested, and if it has been, vote for it. If it's not listed, add it. Tableau regularly reviews Ideas on Community to help determine what features should be added to the product.

TUTORIAL: TABLEAU SERVER COMMAND LINE TOOL

This tool, TABCMD, comes with Tableau Server 8.0 but needs to be installed separately.

Software needed: Tableau Server 8.0. Version 8.0 is used here for consistency in explanation.

INSTALLATION STEPS[21]

The location of the TABCMD Installer will vary depending on operating system.

```
On a 32-bit machine: C:\Program Files\Tableau\Tableau Server\[version]\extras*
On a 64-bit machine: C:\Program Files (x86)\Tableau\Tableau Server\[version]\extras*
```

[version] refers to the version of Tableau Server installed on the machine.

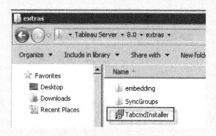

Double-click **TabcmdInstaller** to begin the installation.

According to Tableau's website, the command line utility does not need to be installed on the same machine as Tableau Server. Also, Tableau recommends that tabcmd be installed in your C:\ (i.e., C:\tabcmd).

The installation is fairly straightforward.

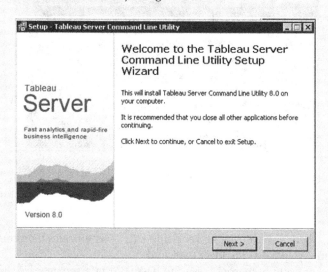

Once tabcmd is installed, open the Command Prompt (as Administrator) from:

Start Menu -> Programs -> Accessories -> Command Prompt (Right-click and select "Run as administrator")

Once the Command Prompt is open, you will need to locate the "tabcmd" tool. This will vary depending on the location of tabcmd.

```
On a 32-bit machine: cd C:\Program Files\Tableau\Tableau Server\[version]\bin
On a 64-bit machine: cd C:\Program Files (x86)\Tableau\Tableau Server\[version]\bin
```

In order to log in to Tableau Server, the first thing you will need to do is login to the server with a user account with the appropriate security access in order to make changes to the dashboards/reports.

```
Administrator: Command Prompt
Microsoft Windows [Version 6.1.7601]
Copyright (c) 2009 Microsoft Corporation.  All rights reserved.

C:\Users\        >cd /D E:\

E:\>cd E:\Program Files (x86)\Tableau\Tableau Server\8.0\bin

E:\Program Files (x86)\Tableau\Tableau Server\8.0\bin>_
```

Normally, the command line to login is:

```
tabcmd login --s http://tableau.company.com --u admin --p password123
```

where - -s specifies server name URL, - -u specifies the user, and - -p specifies the login password.

For security reasons, save the password in a separate file. In a text editor (i.e., Notepad), type your password and save it as *pwd.txt*, in the same folder where the batch file is.

TUTORIAL: USE OF "TABCMD" COMMAND TO CREATE A REPORT

Now, instead of exposing our password, our new command line will use the password file:

```
tabcmd login --s http://tableau.company.com --u admin --password-file pwd.txt
```

Use of "tabcmd" command to create a report[21]

```
tabcmd export "My2013Dashboard/FirstPage?EMPLOYEE_ID=123456" ---fullpdf ---pagelayout
portrait --f "C:\My Reports\Report123456.pdf" ---timeout 300
```

Please note that the Tableau server workbook URL is https://tableau.company.com/views/My2013Dashboard/FirstPage.

The above export command uses ONLY the bold face section of this URL, that is, **My2013Dashboard/FirstPage.**

This is followed by ?EMPLOYEE_ID=123456, which sets the value for the parameter in the workbook. In this case, the report returns the results for the employee with ID number 123456.

- Fullpdf command is used to export a workbook that was published with the sheets as tabs, so this captures and produces the PDF containing all the sheets in the report.

- Pagelayout portrait command sets the page orientation.

- f command provides the file location where the report should be stored.

- Timeout command sets number of seconds the server should wait before processing the login command.

Note: You can point and send the report to any **existing** directory you specify in the command.

TABLEAU TUNING FEATURES

Tableau was designed to facilitate real-time conversations with data across multiple data platforms. Business users who have felt stymied by traditional tools have flocked to this modus operandi. So what happens when queries return in hours or minutes rather than seconds? Can their "flow" be maintained? Thus, it is imperative to provide fast query speeds to keep users engaged so that they can gain more insight from their Big Data deployments.

Users can apply a number of best practices to maximize the performance of their Tableau visualizations and dashboards built on Big Data platforms. The best practices largely fall into five activities.[22]

Fast Interactive Query Engine

We know that HIVE on MapReduce is ideal for ETL batch processing, but it lacks in performance. Outside of HIVE on MapReduce, there are a number of great options for accelerating interactive queries. IMPALA can be used to query a HIVE data warehouse (DWH), and is widely known to have the fastest performance on Hadoop.

For persistent data storage, there are fast analytical databases such as Actian Vector, HP Vertica, Teradata Aster Data, SAP Hana, ParAccel, Pivotal Greenplum, and others that can serve as an excellent place to host business data for low latency queries for Tableau users after it has been processed in Hadoop.

There is also the option to use Amazon Redshift, which is a fully managed columnar storage DWH that focuses on fast data access.

Strategically Utilize Live Connections versus Extracts

We learned earlier how to create live connections in Tableau for a wide range of high-performance databases/data warehouses. These live connections can be effectively used to improve query performance.

Curate Data from the Data Lake

Hadoop's capability to scale its use of inexpensive commodity servers and ability to handle un-structured data makes it ideal for Data Lakes. Tableau is an effective tool for exploring data in the Data Lake, but when you want the best performance for visualization against Hadoop for the knowledge workers to leverage, it is always best to curate the dataset first.

The following steps can be taken to curate the data in the Data Lake:

- Data Partitioning – Organizing a HIVE table into separate files (each with many data blocks) in a distributed system with one or more partitioning fields can greatly accelerate queries over a query that's filtered by a non-partitioned field.

- Dataset Size – When you know the dimensions and measures you want to look at for a set of analysis and the range of records, limiting the ultimate dataset that's exposed to the knowledge workers will always improve performance.

- Clustered Fields as Grouping Fields and Join Keys – Fields that are clustered can dictate how the data in the table is separated on disk. JOINs and GROUP BYs of clustered fields will see improved performance.

- Use of Pre-Joined Views – Creation of materialized views across functional areas to avoid unnecessary run-time joins.

- Storage File Format – File format plays a key role in the efficient execution of queries. Utilize the file format that best matches the query engine being used. For HIVE this is the Optimized Row Columnar (ORC) format, and for IMPALA this is Parquet format.

Optimize Data Extracts

Tableau's data engine is an in-memory analytics database that leverages the complete memory hierarchy from disk to L1 cache. It can be a powerful tool for accelerating your analysis.

- Define Filters – Keep focus on the data of interest.

- Pin frequently used queries in the memory.

- Create selected view to hide unused fields.

- Create materialized view to rollup data to more aggregate dimensions when fine-grained data is not needed.

- Roll-up date dimension to coarser-grained timelines when possible.

- Data sampling can greatly compact the data while still representing the broad trends in the data.

- Following the Top N 80-20 rule, if looking for the highest values in a dataset such as "Sales Revenue," this is an efficient means to reduce the dataset size.

Customize Tableau Connection Performance

Custom SQL – Custom SQL allows for SQL expressions to be used as the basis for a connection in Tableau. Custom SQL can be especially effective for limiting the dataset size (by using the LIMIT clause) so that you can explore or profile a new dataset.

- Initial SQL – Initial SQL provides the ability to set configuration parameters and perform work right when you establish a connection. You can do things such as:

  - Add hints for degree of parallelism in query to increase parallelism for data analysis by reducing the default block size for Maps and Reduces.

  - Optimize join performance by turning on clustered fields.

  - Adjusting configurations for uneven distribution by turning on settings that inform HIVE to take a different approach for MapReduce jobs. These could involve use of reverse indexes for balanced key ranges across index blocks.

CHAPTER 8

Structured and Un-Structured Data Analytics

OVERVIEW

We know that most of the data generated in the Big Data realm is un-structured. Let us see how we will analyze un-structured data. One approach we know is becoming increasingly valued as a way to gain business value from un-structured data is text analytics. As we have seen earlier, the R programming language can be used to perform text analytics. Text analytics is the process of analyzing un-structured text, extracting relevant information, and transforming it into structured information that can then be leveraged in various ways using traditional data processing. The analysis and extraction processes take advantage of techniques that originated in computational linguistics, statistics, and other computer science disciplines.

To get the most business value from our real-time analysis of un-structured data, we need to understand that data in context with historical data on customers, products, transactions, and operations. This real-time analysis has supported the emergence of 3-D dashboards that provide insight into "data we don't know that we need to know." In other words, we will need to integrate the un-structured data with traditional structured data.

Out of necessity to analyze un-structured data, a new discipline of data analytics called data virtualization is born (see Chapter 9). Data virtualization accesses data from different sources and makes sense of it without making copy of it anywhere. These virtual data models are made available as query-driven services for consumption of data by BI tools such as Tableau or direct queries from Apache Spark or Cassandra. The fundamental data virtualization concept is that it can bring data live from multiple sources without having to first put it in a staging database. Anyone who needs data can query this virtual database exactly as if it were a physical database. Thus, we have avoided the processing overhead of bringing data from multiple sources into a staging database, then integrating cross-functional data as pre-joined materialized views for subsequent queries. But, this forced data latency upon us, and we talked about data having issues like 12-hour latency. On the other hand, Data Virtualization delivers real-time data from multiple sources of record that can be made available in a matter of minutes using web services like REST or SOAP. Fortunately, Enterprise Enabler Agile Integration software has come of age as truly enterprise ready technology for both agile analytics and data virtualization.

TEXT ANALYTICS AS MEANS TO EXTRACT VALUE FROM UN-STRUCTURED DATA

Gartner's IT Glossary defines text analytics as the process of deriving information from text sources for purposes that include summarization, classification, investigation, sentiment analysis (the nature of commentary on a topic), and explication (what drives that commentary).

It's essential to understand how this definition translates into action and the value you can generate through the various capabilities of text analytics. These include search and information retrieval, information extraction through techniques such as natural language processing (NLP), tagging or annotation, lexical analysis to study word frequency and distribution, singular value decomposition (SVD), pattern recognition, data mining techniques including link and association analysis, predictive analysis, segmentation, and visualization.

Simply put, without the core capability of converting un-structured text into a structured form, text cannot be analyzed in sophisticated ways. The alternative is a painstakingly manual and error-prone process.

How can text analytics be applied to solve today's business problems? Some of the most powerful applications are in customer service. By analyzing contact center and other voice- or text-based interactions, organizations can understand what customers like and don't like. They can determine the drivers behind customer behavior and anticipate customer needs. They can get to the root causes behind customer complaints and have an early-warning system. With streaming technology enabling on-the-fly analyses, organizations can serve customers, make real-time recommendations to influence behavior, or even detect fraud at the point of interaction.[23]

The Internet of Things (IoT) is driving demand for applications that combine structured data such as operational details with un-structured data such as log files.

MAJOR PLAYERS IN TEXT ANALYTICS

As we know by now, text analytics is complex. But we can't just shy away from its complexity, because it has a wealth of hidden information that is extremely useful for the business. Because of its complexity, we need people from different disciplines to join hands and uncover the hidden business information. The major players in text analytics are listed below.

Decision Maker

This is the most important player. This is the person who applies the results of text analytics to work more productively and to make faster and more informed decisions. This might be a business or product owner, chief customer officer, director of risk management, or head of investigations. These people want the analytics to fit into their workflows and work with the output, drill-down, and explore and understand business patterns.

Domain Expert

This is the subject matter expert. This is the player who solves the mystery by extracting useful business information from the un-structured textual data. In other words, this player is the business analyst who combines in-depth understanding of the application domain with the insights from text analytics to integrate pertinent information into a coherent message. For example, a law enforcement analyst or investigator wants to solve crimes more quickly by connecting the dots from one crime to another, to find the linkages and patterns within the narratives of criminal records without having to read through hundreds or thousands of records. That's why the Federal Bureau of Investigation (FBI) always builds profiles of criminals and saves these in the FBI Vault for future use.

Linguist

This is a player who deciphers un-structured textual data. This player writes linguistic rules and defines corporate taxonomies and lexicons. In practice, many organizations have to compromise on this expertise. Many have seen success with the linguistic responsibility being picked by a domain expert or analyst if a domain-specific taxonomy is available and the goal is primarily text extraction, exploration, categorization, or sentiment analysis, and not using un-structured text in predictive models.

Data Scientists

This is the player who builds the machine learning and statistical models that can be deployed in batch or real-time operational systems. They work with domain experts and business owners to create "gold standards" of documents or other content which can be used as the basis for text analytics models, and they provide checks on the statistical validity of the decisions being made. With the right technology and training the data scientist can develop skills in computational linguistics, which is important to understand and interpret text parsing and related functions.

Conclusion

As you think about this cast of players, keep in mind the interactive and iterative nature of text analytics. To enable these individuals to collaborate regularly and effectively, it's important to equip them with tools and technology that provide out-of-the-box value. Our goal is always to take the complexity out of the text analysis process, while still creating a flexible and scalable environment for a variety of solutions.

FROM DATA TO ACTION

With Big Data getting ever bigger and infiltrating more and more parts of our business, the need for ways to understand the numbers' meaning is becoming more acute. As Tom Davenport of Babson College and MIT writes in Harvard Business Review (HBR), companies must fundamentally rethink how the analysis of data can create value for themselves and their customers.[24]

We'll move beyond specific cases to get at the broader question of how managers can learn to pick the most important kernels of knowledge from the rush of data. Is it critically important for companies' consumer-data teams to have someone who truly understands statistics in a leadership position, or can an untrained manager learn to be more discerning about data?

According to Gartner, the Data Lake is increasingly becoming a mainstream technology. Data Lakes are assisting organizations in expanding their data warehouse environments, giving them the ability to manage more dynamic data volumes. As we mull the pros and cons of deploying a Data Lake, it's important to ensure that our data integration strategy also evolves with our frameworks. Some companies are taking a best-of-breed approach in this way, while others are going ahead with the vendor stack. By courtesy of snapLogic, we outline the top eight data management requirements that businesses must address prior to installing the Data Lake. How well our organization is able to cope with these requirements will decide whether or not our enterprise sinks or swims.

Now we get to the theory, methods, and technology discussion that supports the Top 8 Data Management requirements.[25]

1. Storage and Data Formats

Traditional data warehousing focused on relational databases as the primary data and storage format. A key concept of the Data Lake is the ability to reliably store a large amount of data. Such data volumes are typically much larger than what can be handled in traditional relational databases, or much larger than what can be handled in a cost-effective manner. To this end, the underlying data storage must be scalable and reliable. The Hadoop Distributed File System (HDFS) and associated Hadoop data management tools have matured, and are now the leading data storage technology that enables the reliable persistence of large-scale data. However, other storage and Data Lake products can also provide the data store backend for the Data Lake. Open source systems such as Cassandra, HBase, and MongoDB can provide reliable storage for the Data Lake. Alternatively, cloud-based storage services can also be used as a data store backend. Such services include Amazon S3, Google Cloud Storage, and the Microsoft Azure Blob Store.

Unlike relational databases, Big Data storage does not usually dictate a data storage format. That is, Big Data storage supports arbitrary data formats that are understood by the applications that use the data. For example, data may be stored in CSV, RCFile, ORC, or Parquet, to name a few. In addition, various compression techniques – such as GZip, LZO, and Snappy – can be applied to data files to improve space and network bandwidth utilization. This makes Data Lake storage much more flexible. Multiple formats and compression techniques can be used in the same Data Lake to best support specific data and query requirements.

2. Ingest and Delivery – ODBC/JDBC, REST APIs, Connectors
Data Lakes need mechanisms for getting data into and out of the backend storage platform. In traditional data warehouses, data is inserted and queried using some form of SQL and a database driver, possibly via ODBC or JDBC. While compatibility drivers do exist to access Hadoop data, the variety of data formats requires more flexible tooling to accommodate the different formats. Open source tools such as Sqoop and Flume provide low-level interfaces for pulling in data from relational databases and log data respectively. In addition, custom MapReduce programs and scripts are currently used to import data using RESTful APIs. Commercial tools provide pre-built connectors and a wealth of data formats support to mix and match data sources to data repositories in the Data Lake.

Given the variety of data formats for Hadoop data, a comprehensive schema management tool does not yet exist. HIVE's metastore extended via HCatalog provides a relational schema manager for Hadoop data, yet not all data formats can be described in HCatalog. To date, quite a bit of Hadoop data is defined inside applications themselves, perhaps using JSON, AVRO, RCFile, or Parquet. Just like with data endpoints and data formats, the right commercial tools can help describe the Data Lake and bring to surface the schemas for the end users more readily.

3. Discovery and Preparation
Due to the flexibility of data formats in Hadoop data management tools and other Data Lake backend storage platforms, it is common to dump data into the lake before fully understanding the schema of the data. In fact, a lot of data in the Data Lake may be highly un-structured. In any case, the cost effectiveness of Hadoop data makes it possible to prepare the data after it has been acquired. This is more ELT (extract, load, transform) than traditional ETL (extract, transform, load). However, there is a point at which in order to do useful work with a dataset, the format of the data must be understood.

In the open source ecosystem, discovery and preparation can be done at the command line with scripting languages, such as Python and PIG. Ultimately, native MapReduce jobs, PIG, or HIVE can be used to extract useful data out of semi-structured data. This new, accessible data can be used by further analytic queries or machine-learning algorithms. In addition, the prepared data can be delivered to traditional relational databases so that conventional business intelligence tools can directly query it.

Commercial offerings in the data discovery and basic data preparation space offer web-based interfaces (although some are basic on-premise tools for so-called "data blending") for investigating raw data and then devising strategies for cleansing and pulling out relevant data. Such commercial tools range from "lightweight" spreadsheet-like interfaces to heuristic-based analysis interfaces that help guide data discovery and extraction.

4. Transformations and Analytics

Not only are systems like Hadoop more flexible in the types of data that can be stored, they are also more flexible in the types of queries and computations that need to be performed on the stored data. SQL is a powerful language for querying and transforming relational data, but is not appropriate for queries on non-relational data and for employing iterative machine learning algorithms and other arbitrary computations. Tools like HIVEQL, IMPALA, and Spark execute SQL-like queries in Hadoop ecosystem. However, tools like Cascading, Crunch, and PIG bring more flexible data processing to Hadoop data. Most of these tools are powered by one of the two most widely used data processing engines: MapReduce or Spark streaming. In the Data Lake we see three types of transformations and analytics: simple transformations, analytics queries, and ad hoc computation.

Simple transformations include tasks such as data preparation, data cleansing, and filtering. Analytic queries will be used to provide a summary view of a dataset, perhaps cross-referencing other datasets. Finally, ad hoc computation can be used to support a variety of algorithms, for example, building a search index or classification via machine learning. Such algorithms are often iterative in nature and require several passes over the data.

5. Streaming

Traditional data warehouses support batch analytic queries. However, in the open source ecosystem as well as in commercial products we are seeing a convergence of hybrid batch and streaming architectures. For example, Spark supports both batch processing as well as stream processing with Spark Streaming. Apache Flink is another project aiming to combine batch and stream processing. This is a natural progression because fundamentally, it is possible to use very similar APIs and languages to specify a batch or streaming computation. It is no longer necessary to have two completely disparate systems. In fact, a unified architecture makes it easier to discover different types of data sources.

Hybrid batch and streaming architectures will also prove to be extremely beneficial when it comes to IoT data. Streaming can be used to analyze and react data in real time as well as to ingest data into the Data Lake for batch processing. Modern, high-performance messaging systems such as Apache Kafka (see Figure 8.1) exist. It can be used to help in the unification of batch and streaming. Integration tools can help feed Kafka, process Kafka data in a streaming fashion, and also feed a Data Lake with filtered and aggregated data.

Kafka stores key-value messages that come from many arbitrary processes called **producers.** The data can thereby be partitioned in different "partitions" within different "topics." Within a partition, messages are strictly ordered by their offsets (the position of a message within a partition), and indexed and stored together with a timestamp. Other processes called **consumers** can read messages from partitions. For stream processing, Kafka offers the Streams API that allows writing Java applications that consume data from Kafka and write results back to Kafka.[26]

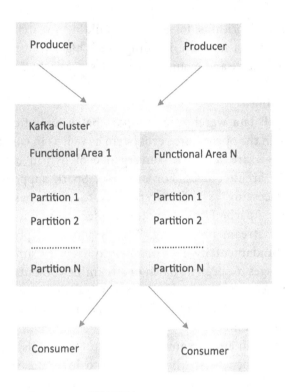

FIGURE 8.1   Overview of KAFKA.

6. Scheduling and Workflow

Orchestration in the Data Lake is a mandatory requirement. Scheduling refers to launching jobs at specified times or in response to an external trigger. Workflow refers to specifying job dependencies and providing a means to execute jobs in a way that the dependencies are respected. A job could be a form of data acquisition, data transformation, or data delivery. In the context of a Data Lake, scheduling and workflow both need to interface with the underlying data storage and data processing platforms. For the enterprise, scheduling and workflow should be defined via a graphical user interface and not through the command line.

The open source ecosystem provides some low-level tools such Oozie, Azkaban, and Luigi. These tools provide command line interfaces and file-based configuration. They are useful mainly for orchestrating work primarily within Hadoop. Commercial data integration tools provide high-level interfaces to scheduling and workflow, making such tasks more accessible to a wider range of IT professionals.

7. Metadata and Governance

Two areas that are still less mature in Data Lake products such as Hadoop are metadata and governance. Metadata refers to updates and access requests as well as schema. These capabilities are provided in the context of the conventional relational data warehouse, where updates are more easily tracked and schema is more constrained.

Work in open source on metadata and governance is progressing, but there is not widespread agreement on a particular implementation. For example, Apache Sentry helps enforce role-based authorization to Hadoop data. It works with some, but not all, Hadoop data management tools.

Enterprises looking to better manage metadata and governance currently employ custom solutions or simply live with limited functionality in this regard. Recently, LinkedIn open sourced an internal tool called <u>WhereHows</u> that may prove to improve the ability to collect, discover, and understand metadata in the Data Lake. Look to see commercial data integration solution providers develop new ways to manage metadata and governance in the enterprise Data Lake.

8. Security

Security in the various Data Lake backends is also evolving and it is addressed at different levels. Hadoop supports Kerberos authentication and UNIX-style authorization as in Lightweight Directory Access Protocol (LDAP) via file and directory permissions. Apache Sentry and Cloudera's Record Service are two approaches to fine-grained authorization within Hadoop data files. There is no universal agreement on an approach to authorization, so consequently not all Hadoop tools support all of the different approaches. This makes it difficult to standardize at the moment because you will restrict the tools that you can use depending on the selected authorization approach.

A lack of a standard makes it difficult for commercial products to provide comprehensive support at this time. However, in the interim, commercial products can serve as a gateway to the Data Lake and provide a good amount of security functionality that can help enterprises meet their security requirements in the short term, then adopt standardized mechanisms as they become available.

CONCLUSION

There is no shortage of hype around the promise of Big Data, the Data Lake, Data Lake products, and the new technologies that are now available to harness the power of the platform. As the market matures, it's going to be increasingly important to begin with the end in mind and build a strategic plan that will scale and grow as our requirements also evolve. Look for a modern data integration provider that has technological depth and breadth in the new world, as well as hands-on experience with enterprise deployments and partnerships. We should not settle for the same old data integration as we build our vision for an enterprise Data Lake to power next-generation analytics and insights.

CHAPTER 9

Data Virtualization

OVERVIEW

The tidal wave of Big Data is here. We need to learn how to slice and dice it and start making superior business decisions. We need to simplify the complexity of Big Data. The Denodo platform presents the technology that provides all the benefits of data virtualization including the ability to provide real-time access to integrated data across an organization's diverse data sources. The data virtualization layer provides the location transparency of data sources whether they originate from on-premise data or data in the cloud. Users access this data without replicating data into any staging database, data mart, or data warehouse. The Denodo platform offers the broadest access to structured and un-structured data residing in a Data Lake comprised of enterprise data, Big Data, and cloud sources in both batch and real-time, exceeding the performance needs of data-intensive organizations.

We have seen how we can capitalize on the value of our enterprise data with infrastructure optimized to deliver actionable, game-changing insights. The key features of data virtualization are enumerated below[27]:

1. Biggest Bang for the Buck

Organizations that apply data virtualization are ones that aim for agile and high-value analytics. These organizations have projects where faster data access and integration will have the biggest impact. Typically, these are organizations that cannot wait for an extended data warehouse development process. They utilize the data virtualization solution that provides a semantic layer. This semantic layer enables integration of metadata for underlying source systems. Using the semantic layer (layer of abstraction), data virtualization masks the complexities of the underlying data sources.

Now, analysts and data scientists can focus on analyzing the data and developing models and algorithms regardless of where the data comes from. In short, the whole idea is to avoid the time and expense of building a data warehouse and loading data into it, only to move data out again into the data marts for data analytics.

2. Enhance Business Analytics Agility with Data Virtualization

In this day and age, agile business analytics is much sought after. Organizations need to harvest data in Data Lakes (see Figure 9.1) so they can explore, cleanse, detect change, shape, enrich data, adjust processes and behavior in response, and be proactive in taking advantage of unanticipated Transforming Data With Intelligence (TDWI) opportunities. Data virtualization can increase an organization's ability to access and integrate data, thereby increasing agility. Agility requires speed; advantages accrue for organizations that can respond quickly to changes in their environment. To do so, business decision makers need to access current, live data for BI visualizations and analytics; they do not have time to wait out traditional data warehousing extraction and loading processes. They may need to develop and run high-performance analytics models and algorithms against multiple data sources (see Figure 9.1) both on-premise or in the cloud.

We cannot overemphasize the point that users do not have to wait for transformation engines to store the results in an intermediate physical database platform, which typically must

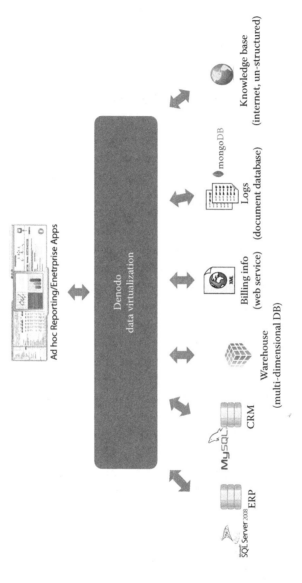

FIGURE 9.1 Denodo data virtualization layer. (From community.denodo.com.)

be preconfigured by IT administrators. Data virtualization can help users interact with data quickly to achieve business agility. Solutions can create virtual views of data coming from live data sources. The underlying complexity is hidden; users don't need to understand how to code queries appropriately for each data source. Once received, the source platforms will interpret and execute queries properly. Data integration can be handled on-demand by defining virtual data marts in the data virtualization layer.

Users have the flexibility to change virtual views as needed for their BI and analytics rather than wait for IT administrators to redo ETL processes and replicate different data. However, now the users do need efficient online connectors to a variety of data sources, both on-premise and in the cloud.

Modern data virtualization solutions can be hosted in the cloud; organizations can take advantage of "Infrastructure as a Service" cloud type where they do not need to manage their virtualization layer on-premise. The virtualization layer can enable organizations to take advantage of the price/performance of processing the data and analytics in the cloud by using the platform's native database system. Because data virtualization can provide location transparency across cloud and on-premises data, users can view data for BI and analytics without needing to know where the data is physically located. For these reasons, organizations should evaluate data virtualization as a means of giving users the flexibility and agility to focus on the business domain rather than the complexities of the data access architecture.

1. Integrate Data Virtualization with Data Cataloging

The concept of a Virtual Master Reference Data as a GOLDEN RECORD has always been important in the BI and analytics domain.

Ideally, the data catalog is a central repository; it contains metadata—that is, descriptive information about datasets from one or more sources, how the datasets are defined, and where to find them. Data virtualization solutions can help by providing services that hook into these catalogs and repositories to assemble a more complete view within one interface. Users can find and preview data through the data virtualization system and apply knowledge about the data coming from the data catalog, glossary, or metadata repository.

With unified views of data and metadata, BI and analytics users can search, query, and discover relevant data and content about customers, products, or other topics of interest more easily and quickly. In this way, data virtualization integrated with data cataloging can help reduce conflicts about who has the correct data. Users can feel more confident when they communicate and collaborate on BI and analytics that they are "speaking the same language."

Shared resources such as data catalogs are critical to improving data quality. One of the biggest sources of delay in analyzing and visualizing data are quality issues, including misspellings, inconsistencies, and false values. With multiple sources including Data Lakes and cloud-based storage, data quality problems can become difficult to manage and resolve. Data virtualization can enable organizations to discover and fix data quality problems, including through the use of profiling.

2. Data Virtualization Provides Ease of Data Governance

Data governance reigns supreme when data proliferates in shape and form across multiple sources and when organizations collect and store potentially sensitive data, including personally identifiable information (PII) about customers, patients, partners, and other entities. There are data governance regulations such as the European Union's General Data Protection Regulations (GDPR), non-compliance of which imposes a penalty on organizations of up to 4% of their annual revenue. Organizations also need policies and practices for tracking and managing other types of sensitive data related to intellectual property, financial information, and strategic plans.

Due to the volume and variety of data across multiple sources, data governance can be challenging. How will data virtualization help?

A semantic layer enables integration of meta-data for underlying source systems. Using the semantic layer (layer of abstraction), data virtualization masks the complexities of the underlying data sources. Organizations can govern entry in one place by using a primary tactic of the semantic layer to provide a single point of entry to the data sources from the BI and analytics tools. Organizations can define integrated access and security policies in the data virtualization layer. They can maintain governance and security authorizations in the layer even as user views change.

See how much better this approach is compared to tracking data access, replication, extraction, and transformation across numerous physical instances (such as data marts, spreadsheets, Data Lakes, and flat files).

Many organizations are extending governance beyond regulatory and security policies to stewardship of the data and ensuring that users and analysts are working with high-quality, trusted, secure data that is consistent and can be shared. Organizations can set up policies and use technologies such as data virtualization and data cataloging to support ongoing efforts to raise the quality and consistency of the data. By eliminating steps for making intermediate, replicated data stores for ETL and other processes, data virtualization can simplify data quality management and stewardship with fewer systems to track and better tracking of user activities.

3. High-Performance BI and Analytics Workloads

Analytics workloads are growing in size, variety, and complexity. Self-service business users and analysts accustomed to simpler BI reporting and descriptive analytics are pushing into predictive and operational analytics to explore what could happen and apply insights that have an immediate impact on operations.

Data scientists are using various techniques and models to predict and prescribe what actions to take to achieve beneficial outcomes and are developing machine learning and other types of algorithms to operate at scale and with autonomy.

Data virtualization, however, can shorten the time it takes to do so because this approach avoids replicating data and creating intermediaté physical data stores (such as data marts, data warehouses, and even Data Lakes) which, although bypassing transformation stages, still require replication and loading of massive quantities of data. It is important to understand how to enable organizations to set up high-performance access to heterogeneous sources.

- *Query optimization*: Data virtualization solutions can apply optimization techniques automatically to accelerate queries. One method used by some solutions is partial aggregation to require fewer returned rows of data, thereby minimizing network traffic. Another technique is to push down processing to the data sources to make the best use of their performance strength, such as when they are built with MPP (massively parallel processing) architecture.

- *In-memory grid*: Some data virtualization systems pair partial aggregation with in-memory MPP for faster post-processing. The grid can be connected to the data virtualization system through a high-speed network to be available when the system needs to post-process large volumes of data.

- *Performance monitoring*: Some data virtualization systems enable organizations to monitor and prioritize workloads to ensure the most important ones perform optimally. Organizations can use workload monitoring capabilities to spot where problems are occurring so that they can remedy them for key BI and analytics projects.

4. Flexible Analytics Application Development

Data-driven organizations want to analyze data generated everywhere: on mobile and edge devices, through their own and partners' channels, and through traditional applications and data systems. This means that application development must be both more diverse and more connected; developers need to employ standard, REST APIs to more easily connect services and components and enable data to flow between them.

Why use REST web services? REST is used because it provides a lighter-weight alternative. Instead of using XML to make a request, REST relies on a simple URL in many cases. Unlike SOAP, REST doesn't have to use XML to provide the response. You can find REST-based web services that output the data in Command Separated Value (CSV), JavaScript Object Notation (JSON), and Really Simple Syndication (RSS). The point is that you can obtain the output you need in a form that's easy to parse within the language you need for your application. In some situations you must provide additional information in special ways, but <u>most web services using REST rely exclusively on obtaining the needed information using the URL approach</u>. REST can use four different HTTP 1.1 verbs (GET, POST, PUT, and DELETE) to perform tasks.

<u>Data virtualization fits with these development trends</u>. Solutions can provide users with real-time logical views of data from multiple sources that could be implementing multiple formats, from traditional ODBC and JDBC to emerging open data services standards such as JSON. JSON is a minimal, readable format for structuring data. It is used primarily to transmit data between a server and web application as an alternative to XML. It works well with REST web services which don't rely on XML.

Having the flexibility of a unified data services layer can be critical to dynamic development of applications and data services. Developers can create applications, such as for marketing departments, that let users find the right data and test analytics models across multiple sources through one interface.

Alternatively, organizations can use data virtualization layers to set up virtual sandboxes specifically for testing models and other programs so that production operational systems are not impacted. The sandboxes can be set up to offer single, virtual views of all data about customers, inventories, or other subjects.

Some data virtualization solutions support the use of application development lifecycle (ALM) tools and apply best practices for version control, governance, security, and other requirements.

Today's data management strategies must match current trends in application development toward agile methods, DevOps, and componentization using microservices (loosely coupled services that use lightweight protocols such as REST). Data virtualization can provide developers and data scientists with the flexibility to shape data management around use of these methods and practices. Data virtualization layers can interface with a variety of data output formats for applications and be customized for specific visualization requirements.

Rather than offer one monolithic enterprise BI or data warehousing system that sets in stone how users will view and interact with result sets no matter how applications are configured, a data virtualization system can offer flexibility. Developers can then fit data consumption to users' preferences, including their use of mobile devices. Developers of data-driven applications need to integrate data models and identify data relationships across heterogeneous data sources. Data virtualization solutions can enable developers and users to visualize data models and relationships from within their chosen data modeling tools. Some data virtualization solutions can import pre-defined external data models; this is useful for organizations that want to incorporate reference models used by their enterprise BI and data warehousing systems, as well as data models used by third-party packaged applications.

Organizations should evaluate data virtualization functionality to ensure that the solution enables developers and users to integrate data models. Such capabilities are critical for organizations that are seeking to break down data silos through better integration, rather than risk adding more silos as they build new applications and data services.

Conclusion: Flexibility and Agility

By establishing a data virtualization layer, organizations can bypass time-consuming and difficult processes for extracting, transforming, and loading data into a data warehouse, Data Lake, or enterprise hub.

This layer can help organizations unify views of data and content from heterogeneous sources, on-premises and in the cloud, while relieving data consumers from the technical complexities of getting data out of each source.

In this way, technology provides both the flexibility and agility. It can help organizations develop and execute high-value analytics that draw on data from multiple sources and fit the demands of a variety of users and types of projects.

Pre-Installation Steps to Set Up Denodo Development Environment

This section, Installation and Bootstrapping, shows the pre-requisites to start using Denodo and instructions for configuring the Denodo environment and starting to play with data virtualization.[29]

1. Install Denodo into a directory (avoid using the %Program Files% folder). This directory will be referred to as <DENODO _ HOME> throughout this tutorial.

2. Copy the MySQL Connector/J to <DENODO _ HOME> /extensions/thirdparty/lib

3. Install and configure the database:

   1. Install MySQL server.

   2. Start MySQL and launch the MySQL Workbench application.

   3. Connect to the MySQL server and then open the <tutorial _ directory>/MySQL/schema.sql script by choosing "Open SQL Script" from the File menu.

   4. Once the script has been opened, click on Execute (you can use any other method to load the database).

   5. After doing this, you should see a new database schema called "acme_crm" with three tables defined (address, client and

client_type). Test MySQL by logging into the acme_crm database with the credentials: acme_user / acme_user

4. Install a web server:
   We are going to use Jetty to run some of the examples in the tutorials:

   1. Go to `<tutorial _ directory>`/jetty and run: `java -jar start.jar` from the command line. If you do not have a Java Virtual Machine installed on your system, you can use the JVM installed with the Denodo platform under `<DENODO _ HOME>`/jre/bin.

   2. Test the billing web service to see if it has been properly deployed, direct the web browser to: http://localhost:8080/billing/services. If successfully deployed, you will see there a list of available services "BillProvider," "AdminService," and "Version," along with their exposed methods and an option to view the WSDL (Web Services Description Language, an XML format for describing network services) descriptor.

This tutorial will incrementally build a set of views in Denodo to learn the basic concepts about data virtualization; it is important to follow each step. At this point, you should have already downloaded the Denodo Express installation package from your user account.

TUTORIAL: DENODO INSTALLATION

The installation package is a *.zip* file. After decompressing (unzip) the package you will see the files shown in the image below: *The installer includes a Java Run Time Environment (JRE), so a previously installed Java is not necessary.*

denodo-installer-cli

jre

denodo-install-6.0.dat

install.exe

installer_cli.bat

To start the installation GUI:

- **Windows OS**: right-click the *install.exe* file and select Run as administrator.

- **Linux OS**: execute *install.sh* as ROOT user

The installer will show up.

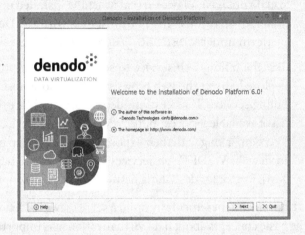

After accepting the terms of the license, you have to select the installation directory (e.g., C:\Denodo\6.0 on Microsoft platform or /opt/denodo/6.0 on Linux platform).

If you already have a Denodo license file, you can select it by clicking on the "Browse" button. Otherwise, you can install the license later from the **Denodo Control Center.**

In the next step you have to select the modules to be installed. This tutorial covers every module so we suggest installing them all, but you only need Virtual DataPort to get started. You can leave the rest of the options with their default values and complete the installation.

Once the installation is complete, you can choose to create a desktop shortcut that can be used to start the **Denodo Control Center**.

If you did not select any Denodo license during the installation process, you can do it from the **Denodo Control Center** when you first start the program. (By first clicking on the **Help** button and then **install license**, a new dialog will be opened to select the license file.)

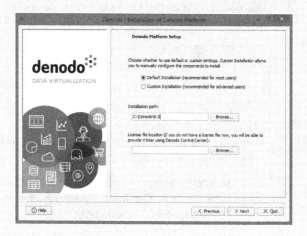

TUTORIAL: DENODO – TABLEAU CONNECTION

This document explains how to configure Denodo and Tableau Desktop to maximize the compatibility between both tools.

Denodo is included as a data source option starting in Tableau 10.4; this native connector simplifies very much the configuration required to enable the connection between Tableau and the Virtual DataPort server.

CREATING THE DENODO DATA SOURCE IN TABLEAU DESKTOP

1. In Tableau, go to Data > New Data Source

2. Select To a Server > More… > Denodo

3. In the Denodo dialog fill in the following fields:

    1. Server: Name of the server where the Virtual DataPort server is running.

    2. Port: ODBC port number, by default it is 9996.

    3. Database: Name of the Denodo virtual database you want to connect to.

    4. Authentication: Select between the authentication methods provided:

        1. Username and Password: Uses standard authentication.

        2. Integrated Authentication: With this option, the adapter will use "Integrated Authentication" (single sign-on) to connect to the Denodo server.

            – **Server:** When using "Integrated authentication," enter the **Fully Qualified Domain Name** of the host where the Denodo server runs.

            – **Database:** The name of the database that has configured the Kerberos authentication for ODBC/ADO.NET connections.

            Before using this option, you need to enable Kerberos authentication for the ODBC interface of the Denodo database you are connecting to.

    5. Select Require SSL if SSL is needed (for proper cybersecurity, SSL should be selected).

    6. Finally, click Sign In.

Defining the ODBC Connection

1. Install the ODBC driver. In Denodo 7.0 and 6.0, you can find the ODBC driver in `<DENODO _ HOME>/tools/ client-drivers/odbc`.

2. To find the details on how to install and configure the ODBC driver, go to the Virtual DataPort Developer Guide section "Configuration of the ODBC Driver in Windows."

3. Create a DSN that points to Denodo, following the instructions described in the Virtual DataPort Developer Guide

4. In the configuration of the DSN, specify the new i18n map. To do so, open the Options > Datasource section, go to Page 2, and add

```
set Connect Settings to "set i18n to
us_pst_tableau".
```

ADD THE TABLEAU CONFIGURATION FILE FOR DENODO DATA SOURCES

Once the DSN to be used from Tableau is defined, to increase the compatibility between Tableau and Denodo, a Tableau configuration file can be defined to set the behavior that Denodo expects in the connections and queries coming from Tableau. The following configuration file can be used: **odbc64-denodo.tdc.**

```xml
<connection-customization class='genericodbc' enabled='true' version='9.3'>
<vendor name='PostgreSQL' />
<driver name='DenodoODBC Unicode(x64)' />
<CUSTOMIZATIONS>
  <customization name='CAP_CREATE_TEMP_TABLES' value='no' />
  <customization name='CAP_ISOLATION_LEVEL_READ_COMMITTED' value='no' />
  <customization name='CAP_ISOLATION_LEVEL_READ_UNCOMMITTED' value='no' />
  <customization name='CAP_ISOLATION_LEVEL_REPEATABLE_READS' value='no' />
  <customization name='CAP_ISOLATION_LEVEL_SERIALIZABLE' value='no' />
  <customization name='CAP_ODBC_BIND_DETECT_ALIAS_CASE_FOLDING' value='no' />
  <customization name='CAP_ODBC_BIND_FORCE_DATETIME_AS_CHAR' value='no' />
  <customization name='CAP_ODBC_BIND_FORCE_DATE_AS_CHAR' value='no' />
  <customization name='CAP_ODBC_BIND_FORCE_MAX_STRING_BUFFERS' value='no' />
  <customization name='CAP_ODBC_BIND_FORCE_MEDIUM_STRING_BUFFERS' value='no' />
  <customization name='CAP_ODBC_BIND_FORCE_SIGNED' value='no' />
  <customization name='CAP_ODBC_BIND_FORCE_SMALL_STRING_BUFFERS' value='no' />
  <customization name='CAP_ODBC_BIND_SUPPRESS_INT64' value='no' />
  <customization name='CAP_ODBC_BIND_SUPPRESS_PREFERRED_TYPES' value='no' />
  <customization name='CAP_ODBC_BIND_SUPPRESS_WIDE_CHAR' value='no' />
  <customization name='CAP_ODBC_CURSOR_DYNAMIC' value='no' />
  <customization name='CAP_ODBC_CURSOR_FORWARD_ONLY' value='no' />
  <customization name='CAP_ODBC_CURSOR_KEYSET_DRIVEN' value='no' />
  <customization name='CAP_ODBC_CURSOR_STATIC' value='no' />
  <customization name='CAP_ODBC_ERROR_IGNORE_FALSE_ALARM' value='no' />
  <customization name='CAP_ODBC_FETCH_BUFFERS_RESIZABLE' value='no' />
```

```xml
<customization name='CAP_ODBC_FETCH_BUFFERS_SIZE_MASSIVE' value='no' />
<customization name='CAP_ODBC_FETCH_CONTINUE_ON_ERROR' value='no' />
<customization name='CAP_ODBC_METADATA_STRING_LENGTH_UNKNOWN' value='no' />
<customization name='CAP_ODBC_METADATA_SUPPRESS_EXECUTED_QUERY' value='no' />
<customization name='CAP_ODBC_METADATA_SUPPRESS_PREPARED_QUERY' value='no' />
<customization name='CAP_ODBC_METADATA_SUPPRESS_SELECT_STAR' value='no' />
<customization name='CAP_ODBC_METADATA_SUPPRESS_SQLCOLUMNS_API' value='no' />
<customization name='CAP_ODBC_METADATA_SUPPRESS_SQLFOREIGNKEYS_API' value='no' />
<customization name='CAP_ODBC_METADATA_SUPPRESS_SQLPRIMARYKEYS_API' value='no' />
<customization name='CAP_ODBC_METADATA_SUPPRESS_SQLSTATISTICS_API' value='no' />
<customization name='CAP_ODBC_REBIND_SKIP_UNBIND' value='no' />
<customization name='CAP_ODBC_TRIM_VARCHAR_PADDING' value='no' />
<customization name='CAP_ODBC_UNBIND_AUTO' value='no' />
<customization name='CAP_ODBC_UNBIND_BATCH' value='no' />
<customization name='CAP_ODBC_UNBIND_EACH' value='no' />
<customization name='CAP_QUERY_BOOLEXPR_TO_INTEXPR' value='yes' />
<customization name='CAP_QUERY_FROM_REQUIRES_ALIAS' value='no' />
<customization name='CAP_QUERY_GROUP_BY_ALIAS' value='no' />
<customization name='CAP_QUERY_GROUP_BY_DEGREE' value='yes' />
<customization name='CAP_QUERY_HAVING_REQUIRES_GROUP_BY' value='no' />
<customization name='CAP_QUERY_HAVING_UNSUPPORTED' value='no' />
<customization name='CAP_QUERY_JOIN_ACROSS_SCHEMAS' value='no' />
<customization name='CAP_QUERY_JOIN_REQUIRES_SCOPE' value='no' />
<customization name='CAP_QUERY_NULL_REQUIRES_CAST' value='no' />
```

```
<customization name='CAP_QUERY_SELECT_ALIASES_SORTED' value='yes' />
<customization name='CAP_QUERY_SORT_BY_DEGREE' value='yes' />
<customization name='CAP_QUERY_SUBQUERIES' value='yes' />
<customization name='CAP_QUERY_SUBQUERIES_WITH_TOP' value='yes' />
<customization name='CAP_QUERY_SUBQUERY_QUERY_CONTEXT' value='no' />
<customization name='CAP_QUERY_TOPSTYLE_LIMIT' value='yes' />
<customization name='CAP_QUERY_TOPSTYLE_ROWNUM' value='no' />
<customization name='CAP_QUERY_TOPSTYLE_TOP' value='no' />
<customization name='CAP_QUERY_TOP_0_METADATA' value='no' />
<customization name='CAP_QUERY_TOP_N' value='yes' />
<customization name='CAP_QUERY_WHERE_FALSE_METADATA' value='no' />
<customization name='CAP_SELECT_INTO' value='no' />
<customization name='CAP_SELECT_TOP_INTO' value='yes' />
<customization name='CAP_SET_ISOLATION_LEVEL_VIA_ODBC_API' value='no' />
<customization name='CAP_SET_ISOLATION_LEVEL_VIA_SQL' value='no' />
<customization name='CAP_SUPPRESS_CONNECTION_POOLING' value='no' />
<customization name='CAP_SUPPRESS_DISCOVERY_QUERIES' value='yes' />
<customization name='SQL_AGGREGATE_FUNCTIONS' value='64' />
<customization name='SQL_CATALOG_NAME_SEPARATOR' value='.' />
<customization name='SQL_CATALOG_TERM' value='catalog' />
<customization name='SQL_CATALOG_USAGE' value='1' />
<customization name='SQL_COLUMN_ALIAS' value='Y' />
<customization name='SQL_CONVERT_BIGINT' value='0' />
<customization name='SQL_CONVERT_BINARY' value='0' />
```

```
<customization name='SQL_CONVERT_BIT' value='4104' />
<customization name='SQL_CONVERT_CHAR' value='0' />
<customization name='SQL_CONVERT_DATE' value='0' />
<customization name='SQL_CONVERT_DECIMAL' value='0' />
<customization name='SQL_CONVERT_DOUBLE' value='0' />
<customization name='SQL_CONVERT_FLOAT' value='0' />
<customization name='SQL_CONVERT_FUNCTIONS' value='1' />
<customization name='SQL_CONVERT_INTEGER' value='4104' />
<customization name='SQL_CONVERT_LONGVARBINARY' value='0' />
<customization name='SQL_CONVERT_NUMERIC' value='0' />
<customization name='SQL_CONVERT_REAL' value='0' />
<customization name='SQL_CONVERT_SMALLINT' value='4104' />
<customization name='SQL_CONVERT_TIME' value='0' />
<customization name='SQL_CONVERT_TIMESTAMP' value='0' />
<customization name='SQL_CONVERT_TINYINT' value='4104' />
<customization name='SQL_CONVERT_VARBINARY' value='0' />
<customization name='SQL_CONVERT_VARCHAR' value='4104' />
<customization name='SQL_CURSOR_COMMIT_BEHAVIOR' value='2' />
<customization name='SQL_DBMS_NAME' value='PostgreSQL' />
<customization name='SQL_DBMS_VER' value='9.0.1' />
<customization name='SQL_DRIVER_ODBC_VER' value='03.51' />
<customization name='SQL_DRIVER_VER' value='09.03.0400' />
<customization name='SQL_IDENTIFIER_QUOTE_CHAR' value='&quot;' />
<customization name='SQL_MAX_IDENTIFIER_LEN' value='64' />
<customization name='SQL_NUMERIC_FUNCTIONS' value='7798783' />
```

```
    <customization name='SQL_ODBC_INTERFACE_CONFORMANCE' value='1' />
    <customization name='SQL_ODBC_VER' value='03.80.0000' />
    <customization name='SQL_OJ_CAPABILITIES' value='127' />
    <customization name='SQL_QUOTED_IDENTIFIER_CASE' value='3' />
    <customization name='SQL_SCHEMA_TERM' value='schema' />
    <customization name='SQL_SCHEMA_USAGE' value='29' />
    <customization name='SQL_SPECIAL_CHARACTERS' value='_' />
    <customization name='SQL_SQL92_DATETIME_FUNCTIONS' value='7' />
    <customization name='SQL_SQL92_NUMERIC_VALUE_FUNCTIONS' value='63' />
    <customization name='SQL_SQL92_PREDICATES' value='16007' />
    <customization name='SQL_SQL92_RELATIONAL_JOIN_OPERATORS' value='1022' />
    <customization name='SQL_SQL92_STRING_FUNCTIONS' value='255' />
    <customization name='SQL_SQL92_VALUE_EXPRESSIONS' value='15' />
    <customization name='SQL_SQL_CONFORMANCE' value='1' />
    <customization name='SQL_STRING_FUNCTIONS' value='3423577' />
    <customization name='SQL_SYSTEM_FUNCTIONS' value='0' />
    <customization name='SQL_TABLE_TERM' value='table' />
    <customization name='SQL_TIMEDATE_ADD_INTERVALS' value='0' />
    <customization name='SQL_TIMEDATE_DIFF_INTERVALS' value='0' />
    <customization name='SQL_TIMEDATE_FUNCTIONS' value='2097151' />
    <customization name='SQL_TXN_CAPABLE' value='2' />
  </CUSTOMIZATIONS>
</CONNECTION-customization>
```

Note: This configuration file has been tested with Tableau 9.3. In order for Tableau to use the customizations in this configuration file, the version number in the header of the file must match the Tableau version, so make sure to replace the version number to match the Tableau installation.

This configuration file can be used for different Denodo and ODBC driver versions with a minor modification in the tag that defines the driver name:

```
<driver name='DenodoODBC Unicode(x64)' />
```

This tag must include the name of the driver as it can be seen in the DSN configuration, for the 32 bit of the version this entry will be:

```
<driver name='DenodoODBC Unicode' />
```

For versions of the Denodo platform previous to 6.0 the complete name of the driver changes and, for instance, for the 64 bit driver the entry must be:

```
<driver name='PostgreSQL Unicode(x64)' />
```

Note that previous versions of Denodo that use the Postgres SQL driver have some limitations.

Once the configuration file is ready it must be copied to the Tableau installation. If the user has access to the global filesystem, copy the file to:

```
<TABLEAU_HOME>/defaults/Datasources
```

We can access the views we created in the Denodo platform from a client tool. In this specific example we will use Tableau to access Denodo through either the JDBC, ODBC, or web services interface. When setting up the ODBC DSN: the first thing we need for Tableau to access Denodo is to create a standard Windows ODBC DSN (see below).

CONNECTION VERIFICATION: CREATE YOUR REPORT IN TABLEAU

Once Tableau is configured to connect to Denodo, a Tableau report can be created:

1. In Tableau, create a new data source using the generic adapter "Other databases (ODBC)"

2. Choose the DSN created in the previous section and click on "Connect"

3. Choose the table or query, and click OK

CONCLUSION

For many organizations, it is critical to have a complete view of the customer, product, or supplier to more effectively manage call centers, R&D initiatives, or supplier management operations. This requires building a metadata layer that builds a 360° view into the relationships across these entities. The Denodo platform's ability to create virtual views of complete customer information in real time has helped customers across telecommunications, technology, finance, and many other industries to significantly grow their business and improve customer satisfaction.

The virtual layer of data abstraction sitting on top of the components of Data Lake along with the interconnectivity of data sources within the Data Lake through the use of connectors that use ODBC/JDBC/REST APIs provides the cost-effective flexibility and agility in business decision making.

CHAPTER 10

Cloud Computing

OVERVIEW

As we have seen, the Data Lakes used in Big Data environments are comprised of data sources that reside in both on-premise as well as in the cloud. No wonder Big Data has a great dependency on cloud computing. Cloud computing, in fact, has come to the rescue of Big Data.

The advantages of cloud computing, to name a few, can be enumerated as follows:

1. Scalability

2. Reliability

3. Affordability

4. Cloud storage services such as Amazon S3 storage

5. Hybrid infrastructure such as co-location facilities

Now, let us look at the various ways in which the cloud computing is coming to the rescue of Big Data:

- The Big Data industry is converging around three principal public cloud providers—Amazon Web Services, Microsoft

Azure, and Google Cloud Platform. Most software vendors are building solutions that operate in all of them. These and other Big Data public cloud providers, including such established Big Data vendors as IBM and Oracle, are offering managed IaaS and PaaS Data Lakes into which customers and partners are encouraged to develop new applications and into which they're migrating legacy applications.[6]

Cloud-based Big Data silo convergence is speeding enterprise time to value. Users are beginning to step up the pace of consolidation of their siloed Big Data assets into public clouds. The growing dominance of public cloud providers is private Big Data architectures. Just as important, Big Data solutions, both cloud-based and the cross-business silos that have heretofore afflicted enterprises' on-premises, are converging into integrated offerings designed to reduce complexity and accelerate time-to-value. More solution providers are providing standardized APIs for simplifying access, accelerating development, and enabling more comprehensive administration throughout their Big Data solution stacks.

- Wikibon forecasts that the overall Big Data analytics market will grow at an 11% annual growth rate by 2027, reaching $103 billion globally. Much of the market growth in later years will be sustained by the adoption of Big Data analytics in internet of things (IoT), mobility, and other edge-computing use cases.

- Most of the legacy applications are still on traditional data platforms. In order to set the stage for growing use of Big Data, one of the challenges is that Big Data migrations take time and bandwidth. By placing enterprise storage systems in co-location facilities with accelerated network connectivity such as AWS Direct Connect or Microsoft's Azure ExpressRoute, machine instances in clouds will be able to access data at the co-location site without forcing a data migration. The initial instances of these deployments, epitomized by early mover NetApp, were created to provide a higher performance alternative to cloud storage services.

A QUICK GLANCE AT CLOUD COMPUTING

There are three types of cloud environments:

1. Software as a Service (SaaS)

2. Platform as a Service (PaaS)

3. Infrastructure as a Service (IaaS)

Software as a Service (SaaS)

In some ways, SaaS is very similar to the old thin-client model of software provision, where clients, in this case usually web browsers, provide the point-of-access to software running on servers. SaaS is the most familiar form of cloud service for consumers. SaaS moves the task of managing software and its deployment to third-party services. Among the most familiar SaaS applications for business are customer relationship management applications like Salesforce, productivity software suites like Google Apps, storage solution brothers like Box and Dropbox, and business intelligence software like Tableau.

Use of SaaS applications tends to reduce the cost of software ownership by removing the need for technical staff to install, manage, and upgrade software, as well as reduce the cost of licensing software. SaaS applications may usually be provided on a subscription model.

As you will observe in Figure 10.1, the users of SaaS environment are typically the higher-level functional end users, not the IT professionals.

Platform as a Service (PaaS)

PaaS functions at a lower level than SaaS, typically providing a platform on which software can be developed and deployed. The application developers or PaaS providers deliver and maintain the PaaS level.

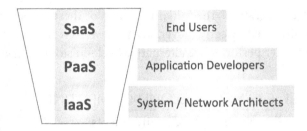

FIGURE 10.1   Cloud computing environment.

The PaaS providers abstract much of the work of dealing with servers and give clients (functional end users) an environment in which the operating system and server software, as well as the underlying server hardware and network infrastructure are taken care of, leaving functional end users free to focus on the business side of scalability and the application development of their product or service.

As with most cloud services, PaaS is built on top of virtualization technology. Businesses can requisition resources as they need them, scaling as demand grows rather than investing in hardware with redundant resources.

Examples of PaaS providers are AWS Elastic Beanstalk, Heroku, Google App Engine, and Red Hat's OpenShift.

Infrastructure as a Service (IaaS)

Moving down the stack, we get to the fundamental building blocks for cloud services. IaaS is comprised of highly automated and scalable compute resources, complemented by cloud storage and network capability which can be self-provisioned, metered, and available on-demand.

As shown in Figure 10.1, IaaS providers are Network and System Architects. They offer these cloud servers and their associated resources via dashboard and/or API. IaaS clients have direct access to their servers and storage just as they would with traditional servers, but gain access to a much higher order of scalability. Users of IaaS can outsource and build a "virtual data center" in the cloud and have access to many of the same technologies and resource capabilities of a traditional data center without having to invest in capacity planning or the physical maintenance and management of it.

IaaS is the most flexible cloud computing model and allows for automated deployment of servers, processing power, storage, and networking. IaaS clients have true control over their infrastructure than users of PaaS or SaaS services. The main uses of IaaS include the actual development and deployment of PaaS, SaaS, and web-scale applications.

There are a lot of providers offering IaaS such as Navisite, Exoscale, and Softlayer, each with their own unique value proposition and service portfolio to choose from.

ComputeNext provides a brokerage service for IaaS so that you can be sure you're choosing the right IaaS provider for your application needs. With normalized access to over 20 cloud providers from a single API, you can compare price and performance across providers to find the best fit – and then build and deploy without getting locked in to just one platform.

IaaS is an instant computing infrastructure that is provisioned and managed over the Internet. Quickly scale up and down with demand, and pay only for what you use.

IaaS helps you avoid the expense and complexity of buying and managing your own physical servers and other data center infrastructure. Each resource is offered as a separate service component, and you only need to rent a particular one for as long as you need it. The cloud computing service provider manages the infrastructure, while you purchase, install, configure, and manage your own software—operating systems, middleware, and applications.

CLOUD COMPUTING VERSUS HADOOP PROCESSING

Many businesses that could benefit from Big Data tasks can't sustain the capital and overhead needed for such an infrastructure. As a result, some organizations rely on public cloud services for Hadoop and MapReduce, which offer enormous scalability.

Cloud computing focuses on on-demand, scalable and adaptable service models such as SaaS, PaaS, and IaaS. Hadoop, on the other hand, is also scalable but is primarily concerned about extracting business value from heaps of structured, semi-structured, and un-structured data.

In cloud computing, Cloud MapReduce is a substitute implementation of MapReduce. The main difference between cloud MapReduce and Hadoop is that Cloud MapReduce doesn't provide its own implementation; rather, it relies on the infrastructure offered by different cloud services providers.

Hadoop is an "ecosystem" of open source software programs which allow cheap computing, which is well distributed on industry-standard hardware and networks. On the other hand, cloud computing is a model where processing and storage resources can be accessed from any location via the Internet.

CLOUD SERVICE MOST SUITED FOR BIG DATA

Infrastructure as a Service (IaaS)

This is the fundamental building block for cloud services. IaaS is comprised of highly automated and scalable compute resources, complemented by cloud storage and network capability which can be self-provisioned, metered, and available on-demand. IaaS providers offer these cloud servers and their associated resources via dashboard and/or API. IaaS clients have direct access to their servers and storage just as they would with traditional servers, but gain access to a much higher order of scalability. Users of IaaS can outsource and build a "virtual data center" in the cloud and have access to many of the same technologies and resource capabilities of a traditional data center without having to invest in capacity planning or the physical maintenance and management of it.

A common business scenario for IaaS is Big Data analytics. Big Data is a popular term for massive datasets that contain potentially valuable patterns, trends, and associations. Mining datasets to locate or uncover these hidden patterns requires a huge amount of processing power, which IaaS economically provides.

Advantages of IaaS

- **Eliminates capital expense and reduces ongoing operation costs.**

- **Improves business continuity and disaster recovery.** With the right service level agreement (SLA) in place, IaaS can reduce this cost and access applications and data as usual during a disaster or outage.

- **Responds quicker to shifting business conditions.** IaaS enables you to quickly scale up resources.

- **Focuses on your core business.** IaaS allows your team to focus on your core business rather than on IT infrastructure.

- **Increases stability, reliability, and supportability.** With the appropriate agreement in place, the service provider assures that your infrastructure is reliable and meets SLAs.

- **Better security.** With the appropriate service agreement, a cloud service provider can provide security for your applications and data that may be better than what you can attain in-house.

CONCLUSION

Cloud computing has the potential to have a great impact on the world. As enumerated above, it has many benefits that it provides to users and businesses. Cloud computing has revolutionized how we protect data at rest as well as data in motion by implementing strict cybersecurity measures. It plays an important role in Big Data solutions, both cloud-based and on-premises. These efforts are converging into integrated offerings designed to reduce complexity and accelerate time-to-value.

Self-Assessment Quiz

1. Why is there this march towards Big Data?
   (a) Large Volume of Data
   (b) Data Complexity
   (c) Existence of IoT, Cloud Computing, and Clustered Servers
   (d) Inefficient Legacy Technology

2. What are the 4V's of Big Data?
   (a) Velocity, Variety, Volume, Veracity
   (b) Vision, Volume, Vertical Schema, Variety
   (c) Virtual Servers, Vertical Schema, Vision, Volume
   (d) Virtual Machines, Vertical Schema, Vision, Volume

3. What factors have set the stage for Big Data?
   (a) Advanced Technology
   (b) Existence of IoT, Cloud Computing, and Clustered Servers
   (c) Inefficient Legacy Technology
   (d) Data Complexity

4. What is Big Data composed of?
   (a) Combination of Structured, Semi-Structured, Un-Structured Data
   (b) Complex Data
   (c) Large Binary Objects
   (d) Large Size Data

5. What drives Business Intelligence?
   (a) Information
   (b) Binary Digital Information
   (c) Business Value
   (d) Quality Data

6. What are the essential components of Big Data implementation?
   (a) Tools and Techniques, Infrastructure, Distributed Processing
   (b) MapReduce
   (c) Hadoop
   (d) Virtual Machines

7. What are the different types of Big Data projects?
   (a) Business Intelligence
   (b) Predictive Analytics
   (c) Storage and Application Driven
   (d) Artificial Intelligence

8. How does Big Data bring great value to the business?
   (a) Better Data Modeling
   (b) Better Data Governance
   (c) Use of Predictive Analysis, Machine Learning, 3-D Dashboards
   (d) Quality Data Analysis

9. What is Hadoop architecture?
   (a) Java Virtual Machine
   (b) Node Cluster and Hadoop Distributed File System
   (c) Distributed Processing
   (d) Interconnected Commodity Servers

10. What are the design considerations for Hadoop cluster?
    (a) Interconnected, Cost-Effective Commodity Servers
    (b) Distributed Storage and Processing Framework
    (c) Java Virtual Machine
    (d) Clustered Servers

11. Which JVM does Hadoop use?
    (a) Windows, Linux, and Mac JVMs
    (b) Java Run Time Interprets Java Byte Code for Varied Operating Systems
    (c) Windows Executable
    (d) Mac Executable

12. What is the relationship between Hadoop and Cloudera?
    (a) Hadoop is a framework whereas Cloudera is a software
    (b) Hadoop is a framework whereas Cloudera provides tools for the Hadoop Ecosystem
    (c) Cloudera provides tools to implement the Hadoop framework
    (d) Hadoop and Cloudera are both software products

13. Where is application data stored in Hadoop Distributed File System (HDFS)?
    (a) DataNode
    (b) Master Node
    (c) NameNode
    (d) Application Node

14. Where is metadata stored in Hadoop Distributed File System (HDFS)?
    (a) DataNode
    (b) Master Node
    (c) NameNode
    (d) Application Node

15. HDFS commands are like Linux O/S commands except they are preceded by?
    (a) hdfs -
    (b) hadoop fs –
    (c) hdfs
    (d) hdfs ++

16. How is data set up in HDFS to support fast and efficient parallel processing?
    (a) MapReduce splits input data over multiple DataNodes in the cluster
    (b) Uses distributed processing
    (c) Performs parallel processing
    (d) MapReduce splits input data over multiple DataNodes and runs in parallel but separately on each node

17. How does MapReduce run on parallel nodes?
    (a) MapReduce splits input data over multiple DataNodes and runs in parallel but separately on each node
    (b) Under Hadoop Version 2, the NameNode and DataNode daemons provide a framework for distributed and parallel data processing
    (c) Use of HDFS
    (d) Use of clustered nodes

18. How does Hadoop process data in a distributed fashion?
    (a) Under Hadoop Version 2, the NameNode and DataNode daemons provide a framework for distributed and parallel data processing
    (b) Use of HDFS
    (c) Use of clustered nodes
    (d) Distributed database

19. What are MapReduce Java classes?
    (a) Splitter and Shuffler
    (b) Mapper, Reducer, and Driver
    (c) Emit, Mapper, and Shuffler
    (d) Emit, Splitter, and Shuffler

20. Does the reducer generate key/value pair, why or why not?
    (a) No, key value pair is generated by Mapper
    (b) No, key value pair is generated by Mapper; Reducer aggregates these to a higher level of data abstraction

(c) Yes, because it is the last step in MapReduce

(d) Yes, because it runs after Splitter and Shuffler

21. Which tool is used to migrate data from Relational D.B to HIVE D.B?

(a) SQOOP

(b) Tableau

(c) IMPALA

(d) HDFS

22. Which ETL tool uses MapReduce to feed data into HIVE D.B?

(a) INFORMATICA

(b) INFORMATICA and PENTAHO

(c) DATASTAGE

(d) AB INITIO

23. What is common between Business Intelligence applications and MapReduce Processing?

(a) Batch Processing

(b) Write Once, Read Many Transactions

(c) Online Transactions

(d) Ad Hoc Reporting

24. How does Sqoop load Oracle table into HIVE DB table?

(a) Import into HIVE

(b) Command Line Interface

(c) GUI

(d) Import which executes MapReduce to load into HIVE

25. How many ways are there to migrate data from Oracle database to HDFS?

(a) Import into HIVE

(b) Import into HIVE and/or HDFS directory

(c) Import which executes MapReduce to load into HIVE and/or HDFS directory

(d) Execute Java program

26. What are the components of the "connect" string from HDFS server to Oracle D.B?
    - (a) IP address of Oracle server, Oracle Listener Port number, Oracle Database Instance name, Oracle system user and password
    - (b) Oracle system user and password
    - (c) IP address of Oracle server, Oracle Listener, Port number, Oracle Database Instance name
    - (d) Oracle Database Instance name

27. Which is the most popular ETL tool used for Data Ingestion into HIVE?
    - (a) INFORMATICA
    - (b) PENTAHO
    - (c) DATASTAGE
    - (d) AB INITIO

28. Why is Tableau the most popular data visualization tool?
    - (a) BI connectors to a wide variety of data sources
    - (b) Handle large datasets
    - (c) Easy to use
    - (d) Built-in graphics

29. How does Type 3 data provide great business value?
    - (a) Data that is already known
    - (b) Data that is known but needs to be known in a different context
    - (c) Data that is not known but needs to be known
    - (d) Data that has business value

30. What type of dashboards use Type 3 data?
    - (a) Fast, wide, and deep dashboards
    - (b) B.I. dashboards
    - (c) Cross-functional dashboards
    - (d) Online dashboards

31. How is cloud technology coming to the rescue of Big Data?
    (a) Providing affordability, scalability, and reliability
    (b) Most businesses cannot sustain the Hadoop infrastructure overhead
    (c) Cloud storage services
    (d) Co-located enterprise storage

32. What is the reason for business to use cloud for their Big Data applications?
    (a) Providing affordability, scalability, and reliability
    (b) Most businesses cannot sustain the Hadoop infrastructure overhead
    (c) Cloud storage services
    (d) Co-located enterprise storage

33. What are the advantages of cloud computing?
    (a) Co-location storage facilities with fast and secure network connections that avoid large-scale data migration
    (b) Most businesses cannot sustain the Hadoop infrastructure overhead
    (c) Providing affordability, scalability, and reliability
    (d) Virtual data center

34. Which cloud service is most suited for Big Data and why?
    (a) Software as a Service because of browser based access to Big Data
    (b) Infrastructure as a Service because of the control to tune the compute, Network and storage capacities
    (c) Platform as a Service because of adaptable service models
    (d) Public cloud service for Hadoop and MapReduce

35. What is agile text analytics?
    (a) Extract value from un-structured data
    (b) Use R programing language

    (c)   Too complex to analyze

    (d)   Text analytics which uses ODBC/JDBC/Web services to connect to text data sources in the data lake

36. What are the advantages of data virtualization?
    (a)   Better data governance
    (b)   Agility and flexibility of data access
    (c)   Works well with Tableau
    (d)   Works well with Denodo

37. How does data virtualization help in data governance?
    (a)   Semantic layer enables integration of metadata for data sources in data lake
    (b)   Better data lineage
    (c)   Single point of entry for data sources in data lake
    (d)   Integrated data security

38. How does Denodo use Tableau?
    (a)   Uses Tableau connectors
    (b)   Creates Denodo data source on Tableau desktop
    (c)   Both are components of Big Data toolset
    (d)   Uses Tableau to drill down during data analytics

39. What type of data analytics are performed in a data lake?
    (a)   Real-time analytics of IoT streaming data
    (b)   Data analysis of data mined in a data mart
    (c)   Text analytics
    (d)   All of the above

40. How do we capture IoT streaming data in real-time?
    (a)   Ingest streaming data into data lake for batch processing
    (b)   Kafka offers Streams API that allows writing Java applications that consume data from Kafka and write results back to Kafka
    (c)   Integrate IoT streaming data with batch
    (d)   All of the above

41. What is text analytics?
    (a) Extract value from un-structured data
    (b) Capturing trends from text data
    (c) Use R programing language
    (d) Too complex to analyze

42. How do we use R programing language?
    (a) Used for natural language processing
    (b) To extract relevant information from text data
    (c) To build fast, wide, and deep dashboards
    (d) To integrate text analytics of the un-structured data in real time

43. How does data virtualization help in reducing processing time?
    (a) By using ODBC/JDBC/REST APIs to connect to data sources in data lake
    (b) By eliminating the need to extract, transform, and load data from source systems into data mart
    (c) By providing high degree of agility and flexibility in accessing data sources in data lake
    (d) All of the above

ANSWERS TO THE SELF-ASSESSMENT QUIZ

Correct answers are boldface

1. Why is there this march towards Big Data?
    (a) Large Volume of Data
    (b) Data Complexity
    (c) **Existence of IoT, Cloud Computing, and Clustered Servers**
    (d) Inefficient Legacy Technology

2. What are the 4V's of Big Data?
    (a) **Velocity, Variety, Volume, Veracity**
    (b) Vision, Volume, Vertical Schema, Variety

    (c)   Virtual Servers, Vertical Schema, Vision, Volume

    (d)   Virtual Machines, Vertical Schema, Vision, Volume

3. What factors have set the stage for Big Data?
   - (a) Advanced Technology
   - (b) **Existence of IoT, Cloud Computing, Clustered Servers**
   - (c) Inefficient Legacy Technology
   - (d) Data Complexity

4. What is Big Data composed of?
   - (a) **Combination of Structured, Semi-Structured, Un-Structured Data**
   - (b) Complex Data
   - (c) Large Binary Objects
   - (d) Large Size Data

5. What drives Business Intelligence?
   - (a) Information
   - (b) Binary Digital Information
   - (c) **Business Value**
   - (d) Quality Data

6. What are the essential components of Big Data implementation?
   - (a) **Tools and Techniques, Infrastructure, Distributed Processing**
   - (b) MapReduce
   - (c) Hadoop
   - (d) Virtual Machines

7. What are the different types of Big Data projects?
   - (a) Business Intelligence
   - (b) Predictive Analytics
   - (c) **Storage and Application Driven**
   - (d) Artificial Intelligence

8. How does Big Data bring great value to the business?
   - (a) Better Data Modeling
   - (b) Better Data Governance

(c) **Use of Predictive Analysis, Machine Learning, 3-D Dashboards**

(d) Quality Data Analysis

9. What is Hadoop architecture?
   (a) Java Virtual Machine
   (b) **Node Cluster and Hadoop Distributed File System**
   (c) Distributed Processing
   (d) Interconnected Commodity Servers

10. What are the design considerations for Hadoop cluster?
    (a) Interconnected, Cost-Effective Commodity Servers
    (b) **Distributed Storage and Processing Framework**
    (c) Java Virtual Machine
    (d) Clustered Servers

11. Which JVM does Hadoop use?
    (a) Windows, Linux, and Mac JVMs
    (b) **Java Run Time Interprets Java Byte Code for Varied Operating Systems**
    (c) Windows Executable
    (d) Mac Executable

12. What is the relationship between Hadoop and Cloudera?
    (a) Hadoop is a framework whereas Cloudera is a software
    (b) Hadoop is a framework whereas Cloudera provides tools for the Hadoop Ecosystem
    (c) **Cloudera provides tools to implement the Hadoop framework**
    (d) Hadoop and Cloudera are both software products

13. Where is application data stored in Hadoop Distributed File System (HDFS)?
    (a) **DataNode**
    (b) Master Node
    (c) NameNode
    (d) Application Node

14. Where is metadata stored in Hadoop Distributed File System (HDFS)?
    (a) DataNode
    (b) Master Node
    (c) **NameNode**
    (d) Application Node

15. HDFS commands are like Linux O/S commands except they are preceded by?
    (a) hdfs -
    (b) **hadoop fs –**
    (c) hdfs
    (d) hdfs ++

16. How is data set up in HDFS to support fast and efficient parallel processing?
    (a) MapReduce splits input data over multiple DataNodes in the cluster
    (b) Uses distributed processing
    (c) Performs parallel processing
    (d) **MapReduce splits input data over multiple DataNodes and runs in parallel but separately on each node**

17. How does MapReduce run on parallel nodes?
    (a) MapReduce splits input data over multiple DataNodes and runs in parallel but separately on each node
    (b) **Under Hadoop Version 2, the NameNode and DataNode daemons provide a framework for distributed and parallel data processing**
    (c) Use of HDFS
    (d) Use of clustered nodes

18. How does Hadoop process data in a distributed fashion?
    (a) **Under Hadoop Version 2, the NameNode and DataNode daemons provide a framework for distributed and parallel data processing**
    (b) Use of HDFS

(c) Use of clustered nodes

(d) Distributed database

19. What are MapReduce Java classes?

(a) Splitter and Shuffler

(b) **Mapper, Reducer, and Driver**

(c) Emit, Mapper, and Shuffler

(d) Emit, Splitter, and Shuffler

20. Does the reducer generate key/value pair, why or why not?

(a) No, key value pair is generated by Mapper

(b) **No, key value pair is generated by Mapper; Reducer aggregates these to a higher level of data abstraction**

(c) Yes, because it is the last step in MapReduce

(d) Yes, because it runs after Splitter and Shuffler.

21. Which tool is used to migrate data from Relational D.B to HIVE D.B?

(a) **SQOOP**

(b) Tableau

(c) IMPALA

(d) HDFS

22. Which ETL tool uses MapReduce to feed data into HIVE D.B?

(a) INFORMATICA

(b) **INFORMATICA and PENTAHO**

(c) DATASTAGE

(d) AB INITIO

23. What is common between Business Intelligence applications and MapReduce Processing?

(a) Batch Processing

(b) **Write Once, Read Many Transactions**

(c) Online transactions

(d) Ad Hoc Reporting

24. How does Sqoop load Oracle table into HIVE D.B table?
    (a) Import into HIVE
    (b) Command Line Interface
    (c) GUI
    (d) **Import which executes MapReduce to load into HIVE**

25. How many ways are there to migrate data from Oracle database to HDFS?
    (a) Import into HIVE
    (b) Import into HIVE and/or HDFS directory
    (c) **Import which executes MapReduce to load into HIVE and/or HDFS directory**
    (d) Execute Java program

26. What are the components of the "connect" string from HDFS server to Oracle D.B?
    (a) **IP address of Oracle server, Oracle Listener Port number, Oracle Database Instance name, Oracle system user and password**
    (b) Oracle system user and password
    (c) IP address of Oracle server, Oracle Listener, Port number, Oracle Database Instance name
    (d) Oracle Database Instance name

27. Which is the most popular ETL tool used for Data Ingestion into HIVE?
    (a) **INFORMATICA**
    (b) PENTAHO
    (c) DATASTAGE
    (d) AB INITIO

28. Why is Tableau the most popular data visualization tool?
    (a) **B.I connectors to a wide variety of data sources**
    (b) Handle large datasets
    (c) Easy to use
    (d) Built-in graphics

29. How does Type 3 data provide great business value?
    (a) Data that is already known
    (b) Data that is known but needs to be known in a different context
    (c) **Data that is not known but needs to be known**
    (d) Data that has business value

30. What type of dashboards use Type 3 data?
    (a) **Fast, wide, and deep dashboards**
    (b) B.I. dashboards
    (c) Cross-functional dashboards
    (d) Online dashboards

31. How is cloud technology coming to the rescue of Big Data?
    (a) **Providing affordability, scalability, and reliability**
    (b) Most businesses cannot sustain the Hadoop infrastructure overhead
    (c) Cloud storage services
    (d) Co-located enterprise storage

32. What is the reason for business to use cloud for their Big Data applications?
    (a) Providing affordability, scalability, and reliability
    (b) **Most businesses cannot sustain the Hadoop infrastructure overhead**
    (c) Cloud storage services
    (d) Co-located enterprise storage

33. What are the advantages of cloud computing?
    (a) **Co-location storage facilities with fast and secure network connections that avoid large-scale data migration**
    (b) Most businesses cannot sustain the Hadoop infrastructure overhead
    (c) Providing affordability, scalability, and reliability
    (d) Virtual data center

34. Which cloud service is most suited for Big Data and why?
    (a) Software as a Service because of browser based access to Big Data
    (b) **Infrastructure as a Service because of the control to tune the compute, Network and storage capacities**
    (c) Platform as a Service because of adaptable service models
    (d) Public cloud service for Hadoop and MapReduce

35. What is agile text analytics?
    (a) Extract value from un-structured data
    (b) Use R programing language
    (c) Too complex to analyze
    (d) **Text analytics which uses ODBC/JDBC/Web services to connect to text data sources in the data lake**

36. What are the advantages of data virtualization?
    (a) Better data governance
    (b) **Agility and flexibility of data access**
    (c) Works well with Tableau
    (d) Works well with Denodo

37. How does data virtualization help in data governance?
    (a) **Semantic layer enables integration of metadata for data sources in data lake**
    (b) Better data lineage
    (c) Single point of entry for data sources in data lake
    (d) Integrated data security

38. How does Denodo use Tableau?
    (a) Uses Tableau connectors
    (b) **Creates Denodo data source on Tableau desktop**
    (c) Both are components of Big Data toolset
    (d) Uses Tableau to drill down during data analytics

39. What type of data analytics are performed in a data lake?
    (a) Real-time analytics of IoT streaming data
    (b) Data analysis of data mined in a data mart

(c) Text analytics
(d) **All of the above**

40. How do we capture IoT streaming data in real-time?
  (a) Ingest streaming data into data lake for batch processing
  (b) Kafka offers Streams API that allows writing Java applications that consume data from Kafka and write results back to Kafka
  (c) Integrate IoT streaming data with batch
  (d) **All of the above**

41. What is text analytics?
  (a) **Extract value from un-structured data**
  (b) Capturing trends from text data
  (c) Use R programing language
  (d) Too complex to analyze

42. How do we use R programing language?
  (a) Used for natural language processing
  (b) **To extract relevant information from text data**
  (c) To build fast, wide, and deep dashboards
  (d) To integrate text analytics of the un-structured data in real time

43. How does data virtualization help in reducing processing time?
  (a) By using ODBC/JDBC/REST APIs to connect to data sources in data lake
  (b) By eliminating the need to extract, transform, and load data from source systems into data mart
  (c) By providing high degree of agility and flexibility in accessing data sources in data lake
  (d) **All of the above**

References

1. Qubole Big Data Activation Report. 2018. https://go.qubole.com/CA---WP---Big-Data-Activation-Report_LP.html
2. Russom, P. 2016. Transforming Data with Intelligence (TDWI). Research Paper. https://tdwi.org/pages/research/tdwi-research-philip-russom.aspx
3. Kagermann, H., Wahlster, W. and Helbig, J. 2013. Recommendations for implementing the strategic initiative Industrie 4.0, Frankfurt/Main. https://www.acatech.de/Publikation/recommendations-for-implementing-the-strategic-initiative-industrie-4-0-final-report-of-the-industrie-4-0-working-group/
4. Data Processing Requirements of Industry 4.0 - Use Cases for Big Data Applications. 2018. https://www.researchgate.net/.../278842272_Data_processing_requirements_of_Industry. Accessed May 14, 2018.
5. Big Data Analytics Use Cases: R/X for Healthcare .... Science Use Cases Video: Joseph Blue on Data Science for the Healthcare Industry. 2017. https://mapr.com › Blog › Use Cases. Accessed February 21, 2017.
6. Infoworld Big Data Analytics Report: The Cloud Fueled Evolution. 2013. https://www.google.com/search?q=Infoworld+Big+Data+Analytics+Report%3A+The+Cloud+Fueled+Evolution&oq=Infoworld+Big+Data+Analytics+Report% &aqs=chrome..69i57.37502j0j4&sourceid=chrome&ie=UTF-8/. Accessed May 2018.
7. *BISP Trainings: Live Training on Business Intelligence Tools.* http://bisptrainings.com/. Accessed April 2018. *BISP Trainings* is an online training provider with the most powerful learning ... Live Training on Business Intelligence Tools.148
8. Informatica Tutorials: ETL Process Flow. https://www.google.com/search?q=informatica+data+flow+diagram. Accessed January 2014.

9. Informatica® Big Data Management (Version 10.1.1) Installation & Configuration Guide. https://kb.informatica.com/proddocs/Product%20Documentation/5/IN_1011_BigDataManagement InstallationandConfigurationGuide_en.pdf. Accessed January 2017.

10. Command line tool and JDBC driver are provided to connect users to Hive. https://hive.apache.org/. Accessed January 2014.

11. *HIVE Installation (Training, Quickstart VM, Hadoop Concepts).* https://community.cloudera.com/. Accessed February 2018.

12. Murray, D.G. 2017. *Fast and Easy Visual Analysis with Tableau Software.* 2nd Edition. Wiley.

13. R Tutorial. https://www.cyclismo.org/tutorial/R/. Accessed January 2017. Learn R from best instructors-Kelly Black.

14. 2018 Gartner Magic Quadrant. https://www.progress.com/. Accessed February 2018.

15. CITO Research sponsored by TIBCO. https://www.citoresearch.com/. Accessed February 2018.

16. Tableau Community Forums. https://community.tableau.com/. Accessed February 2018.

17. How People Use Tableau. https://www.tableau.com/solutions/. Accessed February 2018.

18. https://tableautinkering.wordpress.com/2015/03/29/tinkering-with-data-refresh-auto-refresh/. Accessed February 2018.

19. Feng, J. Best Practices for Tableau and Hadoop. https://community.tableau.com/thread/257837. Accessed February 2018.

20. Create a Data Source with Clipboard Data. https://onlinehelp.tableau.com/current/pro/desktop/en-us/clipboard_datasource.html. Accessed February 2018.

21. Tableau Help. http://onlinehelp.tableausoftware.com/. Accessed February 2018.

22. Fang, J. 5 Best Practices for Tableau & Hadoop. https://www.tableau.com/es-es/.../5-best-practices-tableau-hadoop. Accessed February 2018.

23. Text Analytics: Unlocking the Value of Un-structured Data – International Institute for Analytics. https://www.sas.com/content/dam/SAS/en_us/doc/research2/iia-text-analytics-unlocking-value-unstructured-data-108443.pdf. Accessed February 2018.

24. O'Connell, A. and Frick, W. You've got the information but what does it mean? Welcome to "From Data To Action." https://hbr.org/2013/11/youve-got-the-information-but-what-does-it-mean-welcome-to-from-data-to-action. Accessed February 2018.

25. Maximizing Big Data Value – snapLogic. https://www.google.com/search?q=Maximizing+Big+Data+Value+−+snapLogic&oq=Maximizing+Big+Data+Value+−+snapLogic&aqs=chrome..69i57.2318j0j4&sourceid. Accessed February 2018.
26. Kafka definition – Wikipedia. https://en.wikipedia.org/wiki/Apache_Kafka/. Accessed February 2018.
27. Stodder, D. TDWI Checklist Report. https://tdwi.org/research/list/tdwi-checklist-reports.aspx. Accessed February 2018.
28. DENODO 6.0 Tutorials. https://community.denodo.com/tutorials/6.0/. Accessed February 2018.
29. The Fastest Way to Data Virtualization. https://community.denodo.com/express/. Accessed February 2018.

Index

Printed in the United States
by Baker & Taylor Publisher Services